CUPIDITY

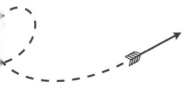

Cupidity

50 stupid things people do for love*

Believing love is a feeling | Believing romance equals love | Standing on your rights | Misunderstanding forgiveness (or refusing to get over it) | Letting the other person's emotions control you | Thinking that telling him everything is a good idea | Trying to fix things | Taking charge | Failing to provide | Fearing the silence | Refusing to grow up | Failing to notice him | Neglecting romance | Loving who you want him to become instead of who he is | Loving who she was instead of who she is | Not accepting his "kills" | Walking on eggshells | Refusing to receive protection or correction | Using sex to get love | Using romance to get sex | Believing sex will keep them | Withholding sex to get romance | Becoming too comfortable with each other | Shacking up | Enabling abuse | Having friends with benefits | Blending finances before marriage | Giving up food to get love

Loving her for her body only | Dressing to get attention | Looking at porn | Having friends of the opposite sex | Giving too much information | Refusing to move forward emotionally | Letting technology define your relationship | Pleasing the other person at all costs | Disrespecting your significant other in public | Refusing to apologize | Not knowing how to break up | Making a big deal out of everything | Having unrealistic expectations | Wishing your significant other were your gender | Loving someone with a different faith | Expecting another person to bring you hope, joy, or peace | Playing god | Obsessing over yourself | Obsessing over them | Rehearsing the other person's faults in your mind | Sharing sins | Not knowing what true love is

*and how to avoid them

HAYLEY & MICHAEL DiMARCO

Tyndale House Publishers, Inc., Carol Stream, Illinois

Visit Tyndale's exciting Web site at www.tyndale.com.

Visit Hungry Planet's Web site at www.hungryplanetbooks.com.

TYNDALE and Tyndale's quill logo are registered trademarks of Tyndale House Publishers, Inc.

Cupidity: 50 Stupid Things People Do for Love and How to Avoid Them

Copyright © 2010 by Hungry Planet, LLC. All rights reserved.

Cover design and interior direction by Hungry Planet

Interior image of mirror copyright © by Kkonkle/iStockphoto. All rights reserved.

Interior designed by Beth Sparkman

Edited by Stephanie Voiland

Published in association with the literary agency of Yates & Yates, LLP, 1100 Town & Country Road, Suite 1300, Orange, CA 92868.

Unless otherwise indicated, all Scripture quotations are taken from the *Holy Bible*, New Living Translation, copyright © 1996, 2004, 2007 by Tyndale House Foundation. Used by permission of Tyndale House Publishers, Inc., Carol Stream, Illinois 60188. All rights reserved.

Scripture quotations marked NIV are taken from the *Holy Bible*, New International Version,® NIV.® Copyright © 1973, 1978, 1984 by Biblica, Inc.™ Used by permission of Zondervan. All rights reserved worldwide.

Scripture quotations marked ESV are from *The Holy Bible*, English Standard Version®, copyright © 2001 by Crossway Bibles, a publishing ministry of Good News Publishers. Used by permission. All rights reserved.

Scripture quotations marked NASB are taken from the *New American Standard Bible*®, copyright © 1960, 1962, 1963, 1968, 1971, 1972, 1973, 1975, 1977, 1995 by The Lockman Foundation. Used by permission.

Library of Congress Cataloging-in-Publication Data

DiMarco, Hayley.
   Cupidity : 50 stupid things people do for love and how to avoid them / Hayley and Michael DiMarco.
      p. cm.
   ISBN 978-1-4143-2467-8 (sc)
   1. Man-woman relationships—Religious aspects—Christianity. 2. Love—Religious aspects—Christianity. I. DiMarco, Michael. II. Title.
   BT705.8.D55 2010
   241'.6765—dc22   2009027422

Printed in the United States of America

16 15 14 13 12 11 10
 7   6   5   4   3   2   1

241. 4765
D. m

To all the stupid things we've done for love,
thanks for nothing!

(Except for this book, of course . . .)

CONTENTS

What Is Cupidity?

Cupidity: where love and stupid meet.

Stupid love—ever experienced it? Ever wished you hadn't? We believe that stupid is as stupid loves. Think stupid thoughts, and end up with a stupid mind. Do stupid things, and, well, you get the picture.

But hey, who hasn't been stupid? Especially in love. We've written over thirty books on relationships and counseled countless individuals about dating issues, and both of us still do stupid stuff in the name of love. So you aren't alone if you realize that you're not the sharpest tool in the shed when it comes to the opposite sex. And even if you have a lot of experience when it comes to relationships, that doesn't mean you can't be reminded and refreshed about the fine art of opposites.

Most of the time when people experience Cupidity, it's because of the lies they've bought and the truth they've not. Stupid lies, like thinking men and women are basically the same. You assume they have the same needs, motivations, and desires, so love should be easy. Just give 'em what *you* want, and you'll get back more of the same. But then you do something like ask him what he's thinking, or you tell her that something she's worried about is "no big deal." And your idea of what the opposite sex is thinking unravels right in front of you.

Hayley:

There was a time, not so long ago, when I thought that if Michael and I got into the car and he didn't start talking, he was mad at me. I was sure his silence meant anger. So I'd get all heated inside, making up all kinds of things I wanted to say about how mean he was or how I hadn't done anything to warrant his being "vengeful." I'd get all worked up for nothing, because the truth is that most guys don't mind silence, and *just because there is no talking, it doesn't mean there's a problem.* Talk about not understanding the opposite sex! ❧

But don't worry—acts of Cupidity aren't disastrous, and they are most often reversible. They're just what some like to call opportunities to "fail forward." Every failure at love is just a chance for you to learn more about what *not* to do. And that's not just the case in dating; the first year of marriage is often full of close-quarters Cupidity. We know a number of couples in healthy, long-term marriages who still fight the urge to love stupidly. Whether you're single or married, you can do a lot to start living on the smart side of love.

Cupidity is not love; it is a cheap imitation of love. It is often entered into as a result of desperation, selfishness, or even self-preservation. It is an attempt to control fate and manage your own destiny through sheer brute strength. Cupidity is born out of the habit of believing love-lies and calling them the truth simply because you've seen them played out in movies or heard your friends swear by them. And because its focus is somewhere on self instead of on the other person, it ultimately leads you to lose out on love.

No matter where you are on the Cupidity scale, we believe that a sober look at some lies you might be buying into will do you some good, both personally and in your relationships. And as a side benefit, it might also give you some perspective in the form of laughter release. Because that's the thing: you've got to laugh at your relational blunders—not while you're in them, of course, but after the dust has settled. Then you can look back at your actions with an eye for change instead of with regret and remorse.

Like the other day, when we started reminiscing about our first year of marriage and how we had to learn how to apologize to each other. Hayley would never say she was sorry, only that something was an accident, or she'd blame the weight of the car door and the wind for slamming it into a pole. Michael, on the other hand, would so instantaneously say, "I'm sorry" that it felt like he was just doing it to move on to something else. Whether it was Hayley's avoidance of the "I.S." phrase or Michael checking the "I.S." box on his to-do list as quickly as possible, we both had to learn what the other person needed to hear when we individually messed up.

Spiritually speaking, Cupidity is choosing to love out of your own self-interest and casting a blind eye to what God says about love and relationships. Essentially, it's believing that God's Word isn't always conducive to love and choosing instead to make your way on your own. Any time you disobey God's Word in the name of "love," you walk right into the Cupidity Café and order up a Cupid-ccino Fail-a-latte. With extra foam.

More often than not, Cupidity is really just stupidity with the best of intentions. Love is the ultimate goal, but Cupidity is just a stupid way of trying to get to it. And what makes it stupid is most often a lack of knowledge. So where do you get knowledge— the good stuff? There are a lot of places you could look. Experts, friends, a former child actor turned reality star . . . everyone has an opinion on love, but there are so many contradictions. How do you get to the truth?

If you've read the Bible, and if you believe the words you've read, then you probably have a pretty good idea of what love is—at least from a grand die-for-you and turn-the-other-cheek perspective. But applying that kind of love to our everyday messy, stinky, and sticky lives is a challenge for us all. The way we look at it, love—true love—is the ultimate removal of self from your definition of love. Love in its genuine form requires a complete focus not just on the wants of the other person but also on their mental, emotional, physical, social, and spiritual *needs*. Imagine how good love would be if no one ever had to search for it themselves—if it were given to each of us freely, with no one manipulating it, using it, or refusing it, and if it were given the way the author of love himself has given it. Imagine if you knew how to love without giving in to your damaged desires and experiences. That would be pretty amazing, huh?

But who are we kidding? This is earth, not heaven, and there are some broken people out there, maybe even right here, reading this book. So love isn't going to be as easy as returning a glass slipper to a perfect little foot and running off in a pumpkin carriage together. Park the gourd and call the podiatrist—there's gonna be some work involved. Smart love will require some painful changes and some refusals to wallow in the misery of it all should your Cupidity lead to heartache. But in the end, a look at the Cupidity in your own life and relationships should at the very least get you thinking and hopefully praying that things can get a whole lot better.

Cupidity Quiz

T F 1. In every (or almost every) relationship you've had, you've heard or had the same complaint.

T F 2. You think and act with your heart instead of your head.

T F 3. You feel like you've "settled" in a relationship.

T F 4. You wish you could change your significant other and make them better suited for you.

T F 5. You've been burned in love.

T F 6. You just can't seem to get over something a significant other did to you in the past.

T F 7. You feel controlled or heavily impacted by your partner's emotions.

T F 8. You don't love yourself enough to love another.

T F 9. You think love is a feeling.

Scoring:

For every *true* you circled, give yourself 2 points: _____

For every *false* you circled, give yourself 1 point: _____

Add up your score: _____

18–13: Hello, Cupid; meet Stupid.

Well, it looks like you've come to the right place. Your love life could use a little vitamin C. And *Cupidity* is here to help. Don't worry—we've all done stupid things in the name of love, but what's really stupid is to keep doing them once you've seen the error of your ways. It's time to take an honest look at how you think and feel about love and make some serious changes to get the stupidity out of your love life.

12–9: Cue the harp music.

You're definitely on the right track when it comes to this love thing. But don't put the book down, because even if you're a good student of love, we've got some new stuff for you to consider. Love is always looking for ways to improve itself, and in these pages that's just what you will find. So let's keep going and discover the subtle nuances of avoiding Cupidity.

Emotional Acts of Cupidity

Believing love is a feeling | Believing romance equals love | Standing on your rights | Misunderstanding forgiveness (or refusing to get over it) | Letting the other person's emotions control you | Thinking that telling him everything is a good idea | Trying to fix things | Taking charge | Failing to provide | Fearing the silence | Refusing to grow up | Failing to notice him | Neglecting romance | Loving who you want him to become instead of who he is | Loving who she was instead of who she is | Not accepting his "kills" | Walking on eggshells | Refusing to receive protection or correction | Using romance to get love | Using romance to get sex | Believing sex will keep them | Withholding sex to get romance | Becoming too comfortable with each other | Shacking up | Enabling abuse | Having friends with benefits | Blending finances before marriage | Giving up food to get love

Loving her for her body only | Dressing to get attention | Looking at porn | Having friends of the opposite sex | Giving too much information | Refusing to move forward emotionally | Letting technology define your relationship | Pleasing the other person at all costs | Disrespecting your significant other in public | Refusing to apologize | Not knowing how to break up | Making a big deal out of everything | Having unrealistic expectations | Wishing your significant other were your gender | Loving someone with a different faith | Expecting another person to bring you hope, joy, or peace | Playing god | Obsessing over yourself | Obsessing over them | Rehearsing the other person's faults in your mind | Sharing sins | Not knowing what true love is

Emotional Acts of Cupidity

Sometimes love is like riding the most extreme roller coaster on the planet and falling off in the middle of the best loop-the-loop. Ouch! Love hurts, there's no doubt. If you've ever fallen into it (or off of it), then you probably have some strong emotions on the subject. And if it's something you've only imagined for your life, then you might have a great sense of excitement about it. But *some-times love isn't all it's cracked up to be*.

The things you've encountered in your love life will naturally color your feelings about the subject and thus your future experiences with it. Feelings—even those nasty little ones you push down and try to bury in the musty recesses of your heart, promising you'll never recall them again—can have a major impact on your love life. So in order to get the Cupidity out and let the real love flow, you've first got to look at your feelings and what they tell you about how you love and receive love.

Feelings are often the first line of defense for your heart. They are often focused inward, like little guards marching back and forth to ward off attack from anything that might injure or steal your heart. But they're also always keeping a lookout for hope, pleasure, and joy. By definition, a feeling is any partly mental, partly physical response marked by pleasure, pain, attraction, or repulsion. And so most often, your feelings either draw you to something or someone, or push you away. Whether you are experiencing an amazing feeling or a horrific one, it will be sent to your brain as an alert, along with a strong recommendation for the next course of action based on its assessment of the situation.

In order to get you to act, **feelings often disguise themselves as reason and thought**. They defend their case based on how many times they've been experienced and how strong the previous experiences were. Even for those of us who deny our feelings or have learned to somehow shut them off, feelings will still go to extreme lengths to manage situations and future experiences. That is why many abuse victims have no memory of past abuse but continue to be affected by it, if only on a subconscious level. Feelings are a powerful force in the life of every human being, and even the lack of emotion is a force that can affect all your actions and reactions to the world around you.

Whether you revel in your emotional life or deny it, your feelings need to be embraced so they can be experienced for what God made them to be and yet guarded to manage the powerful impact they can have on your reason and actions (Proverbs 4:23). **What you feel comes from what you believe.** And for the Christian, what you feel ultimately stems from what you believe to be true about God and his Word, as well as the role God's Word plays in your life. In every situation, you must first run your reactions and emotions by the Word of God. When you do, you will know whether your feelings on a matter can be trusted. Your feelings must have a foundation in faith; only

> *For as he thinks within himself, so he is.* PROVERBS 23:7, NASB

then can they be experienced to their fullest without sin.

When Jesus fell asleep in the middle of the storm (Luke 8:22-25), his feelings were calm and secure. But the emotions of the disciples were anything but—they feared and they worried and finally they complained to the peaceful, sleeping Jesus. So what made the difference in their emotional reactions to the same situation? Their beliefs. Jesus believed that God was his protector and that nothing could touch him except what the Father allowed.

While the disciples might have had head knowledge of this fact, they failed to own it and make it a filter for their emotional lives.

If you look carefully into the perfect law that sets you free, and if you do what it says and don't forget what you heard, then God will bless you for doing it. JAMES 1:25

Emotions are not a ball and chain. They don't need to be avoided or feared; they are a part of the life of a believer just as they were a part of the life of Jesus. While on earth Jesus wept and mourned. He was angry and joyful. He loved deeply and felt great compassion. His feelings weren't hidden, but they were holy—aligned with the truth. If your emotions call you to do anything that goes against God's Word, then they are leading you to acts of foolishness. But if you can filter all you feel, and learn to participate only in emotions that have been made holy, then you can remove the Cupidity from your life and your love.

When it comes to relationships, most of us have a set of principles or ideals we live by, either consciously or subconsciously. Those ideals affect how we react to and treat others who are in relationships with us. Not only that, but they also affect how we are viewed by others and ultimately treated by them. In the life of a believer in love, it is important to understand God's commands regarding relationships here on earth. We are setting ourselves up

The Emotional Life of Jesus

ANGER "He looked around at them angrily and was deeply saddened" *(Mark 3:5)*.

"He was angry with his disciples" *(Mark 10:14)*.

GRIEF "He was deeply troubled. . . . Then Jesus wept" *(John 11:33, 35)*.

"As he came closer to Jerusalem and saw the city ahead, he began to weep" *(Luke 19:41)*.

ANGUISH "I am under a heavy burden" *(Luke 12:50)*.

"He became anguished and distressed" *(Matthew 26:37)*.

COMPASSION "His heart overflowed with compassion" *(Luke 7:13)*.

"Moved with compassion, Jesus reached out and touched him" *(Mark 1:41)*.

JOY "Jesus was filled with the joy of the Holy Spirit" *(Luke 10:21)*.

"I have told you these things so that you will be filled with my joy" *(John 15:11)*.

TEMPTATION "This High Priest of ours understands our weaknesses, for he faced all of the same testings we do, yet he did not sin" *(Hebrews 4:15)*.

for utter disaster if we do anything else. So let's dive into a few emotional acts of Cupidity so we can learn to run our emotional lives through the filter of God's truth instead of the world's.

1

Believing Love
Is a Feeling

One of the biggest acts of Cupidity is to believe that love is a feeling and nothing more. While certainly it is true that love elicits some strong emotions, *love itself isn't a feeling*.

Let's say someone makes you feel amazing. You can't quit thinking about the person, and you are sure that it is love. So you confess your undying love to the object of your affection. Then a few days, a few months, or a few years down the road, that amazing feeling goes away. Does that mean you never loved the person or you stopped loving them? Or does it mean that feelings of love can't be an indicator of the existence of love? It has to be one or the other. Which one you choose says a lot about your core beliefs about love.

Early on in a relationship, it is easy for things other than love to mimic love and cause people to believe they have found their dream come true. There are so many other things that feel just like love. Take jumping out of an airplane, for example. The rush, the adrenaline, the fear, and even the pleasure of that specific moment can have the same emotional reaction and payoff as love's first expression. But obviously, jumping from extreme heights is more about fear and adrenaline than eternal commitment. **A guy can feel the same kinds of emotions for his car as he does for his girl.** *And a woman can feel the same kind of euphoric rush when she buys a pair of shoes as when her man brings her flowers.* But that doesn't mean it's accurate to call those passions love.

Hayley:

In two different relationships before I got married, I committed to making it work based on the feeling that this was the only "good guy" who would love me. Fear was my compelling emotion—I was afraid I couldn't do any better. *I saw the warning signs* in each relationship, but out of fear I chose to overlook them instead of doing a faithful inspection of the problems.

A lot of single people commit Cupidity when they get so wrapped up in the emotion of love that they neglect the truth about love. They ignore red flags, concerns of friends and family, and even warnings from the very object of their love. A well-known Christian counselor once said, "Don't marry the person you think you can live with; marry only the individual you think you can't live without." And while he is no doubt a smart man and that sounds like romantic and sound advice, have you ever considered how many people marry someone they "can't live without," and then four years later they divorce the same person they no longer can live with? Did things fall apart because their way of choosing, based on a feeling, was wrong? Or was it because their definition of love as needing to feel a certain way was faulty? We could answer that for you, but we're not going to. Let's just say that no matter what the answer is, judging the presence of love based on how you feel is a dangerous, er, proposal.

If you are honest with yourself, **would you say that you feel your way through love?** Did you (or would you) choose your mate based on how they make you feel? Have you rejected someone because your feelings changed? Do you consider feelings the best indicator of success or failure in a relationship? Though feelings should be noted, they can't be followed blindly, because when they are, they overshadow God's commands.

Many women can be heard to say things like, "He just doesn't love me anymore." And what they often mean is, "He doesn't make me feel the same way anymore." We've considered that idea a lot. Because we were head over heels in love when we were dating and got married, and since then there have been fewer and fewer of those emotional highs. In fact, we've gone weeks, even months, without them. And the questions that keep lurking are, *Does he love me anymore? Did she ever love me?* But then, being the practical souls we are, we thought about how hard life would be if we permanently felt the same emotional high that we felt in the beginning of the relationship. How would we get any sleep, living in the same house together? When would we remove our lips from each other long enough to eat? How would we concentrate at work when all we could do was imagine being with the other person? That initial feeling of love that is so fantastical is also distracting—nay, *all consuming.* It's your soul's occupation, and while a busy soul is a happy soul, it's also a pleasure-driven soul, finding little strength or focus for things other than true love. We aren't dissing the amazing sensation of "love's first kiss," as our three-year-old fairy tale–loving daughter puts it, but we are saying that it can be a bit of an obsession.

In relationships—especially at the beginning—it is easy to take the incredible emotions another person brings you to as *a sure sign that love is in the air*...when all it might be is the thrill of the chase or the excitement of a mystery waiting to be unraveled. So that brings us back to the original premise that love isn't a feeling but an action. How do we know? Because God commands it. All over Scripture God commands us to love. Love God, love our neighbors as ourselves, even love our enemies. But if love were a feeling, then God couldn't command it. No one can order you to feel something. Emotions don't work like that—you don't turn them on and off, on command. But actions can be commanded: "Share your toys." "Don't hit back!" "Don't touch that" (not to be confused with, "You can't touch this").

> *Love your enemies! Pray for those who persecute you!...If you love only those who love you, what reward is there for that?*
>
> MATTHEW 5:44, 46

But maybe there's more to it than even that. Have you considered why God gave us the command to love in the first place? If love came naturally to all of us, if it were always our first response to all people, in all situations, then God wouldn't have had to make it the focus of his instructions to us (1 Corinthians 16:14). God sees the need to command us to love, because love isn't usually our first response, except when we are deep in it. In those situations, love is easy, natural—like second nature. Love is your "soul" focus: that person gets all the best of you. You are patient, kind, caring, and selfless, and you overlook faults. You are the perfect picture of love in human form. Wow! But God knows us better than that. He knows that love, in order to prove itself true, must be tested. It must stand in the face of opposition (Matthew 5:44); it must give of itself even when it gets nothing in return (Luke 6:35); it must be a conscious choice and not an emotional response (Matthew 5:46).

According to a poll taken in March 2008 by the Barna Research Group, the divorce rate for Christian couples is statistically identical to all other faith groups, as well as atheists and agnostics. Whether or not the Christians polled truly lived biblical lives is questionable—we have no way of knowing their hearts or their basis for calling themselves Christians. But as a random poll of people who consider themselves "saved," this seems to be confirmation that feelings, not faith, most profoundly affect the actions of those who consider themselves faithful.

When you feel your way through love, you are apt to ignore the warning signs that signal a future of difficulty, if not pain. They might even be signs from God that this person is not *the* person. So emotions can't be allowed to have the final say on who you choose.

For the married person, trials and emotionally difficult experiences are part of the pattern of love. These trials—these tests of faith and love—are what

> *Most important of all, continue to show deep love for each other, for love covers a multitude of sins.* 1 PETER 4:8

lead to sanctification, the purification of your faith. Every time a trial rears its evil head, your first question should be *What does God want me to learn about my sin from this?* not *What is my spouse's sin in this?* According to pastor and teacher James MacDonald, **"God's goal is not to make you happy; it's to make you holy."**

When love is based on a feeling, you have Cupidity: stupid, stupid actions taken to try to get more love. But when love is based on actions, you actually get amazing feelings *after* you give in fully to the kind of self-sacrificing love that Jesus taught us through his life. See, when love is patient, kind, humble, meek, and all the other things Jesus taught, it is at its best. And the most amazing thing is that it isn't based on what others do or fail to do. It isn't dependent on situations but on an immovable and perfect God. In short, it's heavenly. Harp music, please!

So we've established that love is an action, not a feeling. But what does that look like? Love is an action not in the sense of "start the film rolling" but in the sense of "it's not what you feel; it's what you do." When you look at it like that, suddenly love becomes less about how people make you feel or what they do to you, but what *you* do in response to them.

Wait a minute . . . you mean love isn't about how a person makes me feel but about how I treat them? Yep, that's it in a nutshell—good job. So if love is lacking in your life, it isn't because of the other person; it's because of you. Ouch, that hurts even as it's coming out. Let's walk through this together—it's too scary alone. According to Scripture, you aren't going to be judged based on the love you feel but the love you give: "Love is patient and kind. Love is not jealous or boastful or proud or rude. It does not demand its own way. It is not irritable, and it keeps no record of being wronged. It does not rejoice about injustice but rejoices whenever the truth wins out. Love never gives up, never loses faith, is always hopeful, and endures through every circumstance" (1 Corinthians 13:4-7). Can't speak for you, but we speak for ourselves when we say that most of these things—like patience, humility, not insisting on getting our own way, never giving up, and enduring all things—ain't

The Way to a Man's Heart Is through His Left Ear

When it comes to helping your beloved know how much you love them, make sure **you speak into their left ear**. According to research in the Times (April 25, 2008), we remember emotional messages best when we hear them through the left ear. On the other hand (or the other side of the head), the right ear is the one you want if you are teaching, giving directions, or sharing nonemotional information. It all has to do with the different functions of the right and left hemispheres of the brain—the left side controls the right side of the body, while the right side of the brain controls the left side of the body.

When you consider that the left part of the brain is the logical side and the right side is more imaginative, it all starts to make sense. **Want to capture someone's imagination or emotions? Then whisper into their left ear.**

In fact, further research suggests that the best cheek for kissing is the left one, and women tend to favor the left side for holding babies. (No research yet if conservative candidates kiss babies on the right cheek while liberals smooch on the left!)

what we originally had in mind when we thought about what love should *feel* like.

Hayley:

Finding Fabio Unshaven in a White T-Shirt

Let me just jump in here. One day I was bemoaning the fact that the romance was gone from our marriage. Because romance is how a woman knows for sure that a man loves her—crazy, I know, but blame it on Disney. Anyway, that day I took to heart God's command to love regardless of what I was getting. I took the time to notice that God is love (1 John 4:16), and my thoughts and actions of love given to my "undeserving" husband transported God's very presence into my life. It was as if my act of obedience produced love and romance, right then and there (1 Thessalonians 3:12; 1 John 4:11-12). And suddenly I thought that Michael was the dreamiest man on the planet. His unshaven face, white T-shirts, and holey socks were all just as they should be. Poor guy—he had no idea what I was going through or why I was so difficult to live with. It was my own misguided ideas of how things should be that made me crazy and caused me to consider him "undeserving" of my love. But when I saw things from God's perspective, *all the smoke cleared and I could see true love.*

It wasn't what I was feeling about Michael but what I believed about God and who he commands me to be that counted. (BTW, Michael is currently editing this unshaven in a white T-shirt.)

If you base your love on how you feel about the other person, then stop the Cupidity now and absorb this truth into your pores. Steam over it. And let the truth set you free. Love, when given God's way, is better and more lasting than any visceral reaction to your dream girl or guy.

Of course, it would be a potential act of Cupidity for a single person to determine that there need be no sensation of love that comes out of interacting with the future Mr. or Mrs. Perfect, whether physically, mentally, or spiritually. There needs to be some kind of chemistry in order to seal the deal and proceed around the proverbial bases, but once you've slid into home (and by that we mean walked down the aisle), how you feel can't determine how much love you give your spouse. But until you marry, you are free to say, "I'm not in love with you, so I'm walking away." You just can't do that once you say, "I do."

So let's just say, enjoy the feeling of love when it comes, but know that *love doesn't have to feel good in order to exist*. Consider Christ on the cross. Certainly this perfect act of love didn't give him the amazing feeling that we associate with true love. In Christ's life, love hurt, to put it mildly. But thank God he knew the hurt that had to be endured in order for love to become available to all of us.

Don't look out only for your own interests, but take an interest in others, too. PHILIPPIANS 2:4

Love demands a lot of us. It demands an end to asking, "What about me?" and requires a search for the answer to "What about the other person? What do they need that I can give?" Anything that doesn't agree with the way God's Word defines love needs to be deleted from your memory. Then you'll be able to start over with a fresh motherboard of love. When you learn to love God's way, you learn to love without Cupidity, and that's a pretty amazing thing.

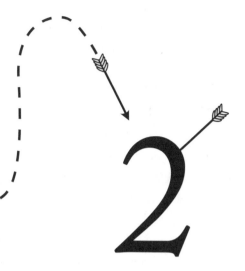

2

Believing Romance Equals Love

As Hayley confessed earlier, for many people (especially the half that tend to wear skirts and high heels), romance is love. Or at least it is a good sign that love is in the air. Without romance, most women have no sense of affection and see no hope for a future with a man. To a woman, romance is a man's attempt to prove to her that she is more than he ever dreamed of and that her very presence makes him feel so much love that he has to shower her with tokens of that love to keep from exploding with joy. Romance in itself isn't a bad thing, and it's true there is a degree of mutual satisfaction when romance is present. But Cupidity comes to visit when a woman receives romance and immediately deduces that it must be love.

There are single men the world over who know the value of romance in the economy of love. They know where it can take them and what it can do for them. And there are a lot of scoundrels who will use it to get what they want. By nature men are not prone to desire romance. So romance most often involves a man attempting to do what makes a woman happy. And that is a noble thing, as long as the man understands that romance means love to the average woman. When a man doesn't realize this or knows it and offers romance even if he isn't interested in the love it will generate, he is acting out of Cupidity. **Romance isn't something a man ought to trifle with.** The word *tease* is often thrown around to describe a girl who leads a guy on, and it might well be used for a guy who leads a girl on through romantic expressions with no love to support it. Everyone knows that being a sexual player is downright shady. But it's also crucial to understand that being a player at the game of romance can be just as harmful. So romancer beware!

Now as far as women are concerned: you know that romance can be a powerful thing in your life. But if you let it influence your heart too much, you'll be living more in the land of Cupidity than sanity. *Romance is like a drug*; you can get addicted and start demanding it in all kinds of places, like your clothes, your home decor, your bedding, and your love life. If you find yourself feeling incomplete and depressed after paging through the Pottery Barn catalog because you don't have the Madison armchair or the Tatum organic duvet cover, then we feel pretty comfortable saying you have some romance issues. (Michael here. My manhood insists that I identify Hayley as the source of that catalog info.) It's like this: romance is a fun ride—it can be rewarding and exciting—but it can't be your entire life. And if you feel sad because you don't have the kind of romance you imagined, then you are giving it too much importance in your life. Obsessing over a lack of romance in any area of your life is one of the ways romance can be equated with love. You buy into the lie that without it you are missing the most important thing in the world.

The problem is clear for single women who equate romance

with love. They run the danger of falling for a smooth, well-placed line or a fancy box of chocolates, and they can easily make themselves depressed over the void of such things in their lives. Romance should be seen as the icing on the cake, the gift with the purchase—not the reason you went to the store in the first place. The single woman would do better to consider the value of romance as an extra but not an essential part of her life. Romance shouldn't be feared or avoided, but it also shouldn't be allowed to dominate her needs list. Romance is not a biblical mandate or a spiritual guarantee, so she shouldn't decide her life is worthless without it. It can make her life beautiful when she finds it, but it's not oxygen.

Romance for the married woman comes with its own warning label. She needs to beware of saying something like, "If there is no romance, then he doesn't love me anymore." Men are hunters; they chase, track, and shoot whatever it is they want, and then when they drag it home, they don't want to keep chasing it. They've done their job. They've romanced their wives and caught them, and now they can finally rest. The hard work is over—at least that's their thought pattern. A husband's lack of romance isn't a sign of his lack of love but of his lack of need. Most likely he just doesn't feel a need for the stuff. That doesn't mean he shouldn't give it, and we'll get to that in a bit, but it does mean that his wife doesn't need to be angry with him or resent him for the sudden change of the status quo. Romance can be exhausting to the man who has to conjure it up. We know, a woman wants it to be effortless—a part of his very fiber—but it's work, hard work, and that's in part what makes it so amazing. She would do well to consider not just the end result but also all the effort and thought he puts into pleasing her. It should please her.

Sometimes part of our hang-up about romance is that our definition of it is too narrow. True romance is something a woman can find regardless of the presence or absence of a significant other in her life. Take a look at a bloodred sunset, and try not to feel the power of the romantic. Feel the cool breeze on your face and hear the leaves rustle as the same wind dances with them, and try not to sense the hand of God in the world around you. ***Romance isn't reserved just for those in exclusive relationships***; it's the echo of an intimate relationship with the very creator of the earth around you.

Romance is there to be had, if only you are willing to change your thoughts from Cupidity to reality. In Philippians, the apostle Paul tells us the secret to real romance when he says, "Fix your thoughts on what is true, and honorable, and right, and pure, and lovely, and admirable. Think about things that are excellent and worthy of praise. Keep putting into practice all you learned and received from me—everything you heard from me and saw me doing. Then the God of peace will be with you" (4:8-9). If the God of peace being right there with you isn't the stuff of true romance, then what is?

Romance can be yours in many ways, so don't bemoan the lack of it in your daily routine. Instead, find joy in it as it arrives unexpectedly. The less you stress about your lack of romance and the more you understand about what it really is, the more you will find it present. Pressure and manipulation never create romance, but rest and faith give it a fertile ground in which to grow.

Top Seven Things Women Think Are Romantic

- *love notes*
- *music mixes*
- *flowers*
- *surprise picnics*
- *cuddling*
- *dancing under the stars*
- *shopping together*

❤ ❤ ❤ ❤ ❤

Top Seven Things Men Think Are Romantic

- seats on the 50–yard line
- a 1966 Mustang
- an Xbox 360
- power tools with a bow or ribbon
- sex (bow or ribbon optional)
- baked goods
- silence

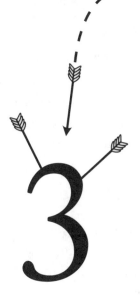

3

Standing on Your Rights

The Founding Fathers of the United States said we have certain inalienable rights: the rights to life, liberty, and the pursuit of happiness. Unfortunately those rights aren't so inalienable when it comes to love. We'll skip over the first two for the purposes of Cupidity and dive right into happiness.

Happiness: you gotta love it. Happiness is the best state to live in. Tennessee and Oregon are tied for second. No sales tax in Oregon, and no income tax in Tennessee . . . but we digress. Is the pursuit of happiness your right, like the Declaration of Independence says? As a citizen of this country it may be, but as a person in love, standing on your rights is an act of emotional Cupidity. **Rights and love don't mix.** (Unless it is the right to initiate the action of love, in which case it's a dandy. Or the right not to be abused, and that should go without saying.) But for the purposes of our discussion here, let's talk about those other rights we think we have in a relationship that can wreak havoc on love.

Think about the guy who falls in love but demands the right to his freedom. He refuses to give up that right, no matter how much he loves her or how much she wants his commitment. Or what about the woman who stands on her right to change her mind at will or be mean when stricken with PMS? If you stop for a sec and just give it some thought, you'll probably come up with a list of rights that you've subconsciously been living by.

I have the right to:

- make you clean up after yourself
- have the toilet seat down
- have dinner on the table at exactly 6 p.m.
- watch every televised game if the opponent is ranked
- have a matching purse for every pair of shoes
- spend my money however I want to

Okay, so maybe none of those rights are on your list. But if there has ever been a time when you told yourself, *I deserve . . .* , *I should have . . .* , or *They ought to . . .* , you've just uncovered your relational Declaration of Independence. Love is anything but independence. It is interdependence.

Even in relationship to God, we are not independent. We definitely don't stand on a list of rights; we stand on a list of commandments. God's Word defines love based not on what we get out of it but on what we give. Therefore, standing on our rights is standing anywhere but in the vicinity of love. "We know what real love is because Jesus gave up his life for us. So we also ought to give up our lives for our brothers and sisters" (1 John 3:16).

At the moment we start standing on our rights—the right to be heard, the right to have things the way we want them, the right to be who we are even if it hurts those we love—that is the moment we stop loving and start taking. Standing on your rights means making demands of love. *And at the moment love makes*

demands, it dies. "This is my commandment: Love each other in the same way I have loved you. There is no greater love than to lay down one's life for one's friends" (John 15:12-13). The thing that *should* die in order for love to grow is our list of rights. To stop standing on your rights is to offer unconditional love.

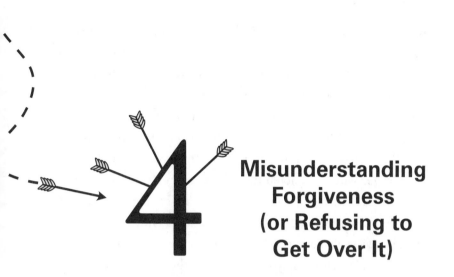

Misunderstanding Forgiveness (or Refusing to Get Over It)

If there is something, anything, you can't get over, then say hello to Cupidity, because it has moved in. When your heart holds something against another person, it becomes fertile ground for all kinds of emotional weeds like bitterness, fear, resentment, anger, dissension . . . and the list goes on. If you suffer from any of those emotions, your suffering is *self-inflicted.* Yes, we just said what you thought we said. Holding on to any sin—your own or someone else's—is basically choosing to carry a load that God wants you to have no part of. Why would you drag around a weight like that when you should just throw it out with the garbage?

Living with unforgiveness in your life can eat you alive emotionally and wound you spiritually. In Matthew 18:21-35, Jesus tells the story of the unforgiving servant. This servant was called before the king, to whom he owed some 193,000 years' worth of wages. The king was mad and wanted his money paid back. But after some begging and pleading on the servant's part, the king forgave him and sent him away debt free. On his way home the forgiven man met a man who owed him some money—about three months' worth of wages—and went off on him, demanding that he pay him what was owed. When the man said he couldn't, the forgiven guy called the cops on his friend and had him arrested for his inability to pay. "When some of the other servants saw this, they were very upset. They went to the king and told him everything that had happened. Then the king called in the man he had forgiven and said, 'You evil servant! I forgave you that tremendous debt because you pleaded with me. Shouldn't you have mercy on your fellow servant, just as I had mercy on you?' Then the angry king sent the man to prison to be tortured until he had paid his entire debt. That's what my heavenly Father will do to you if you refuse to forgive your brothers and sisters from your heart" (Matthew 18:31-35).

Ay, Chihuahua, **unforgiveness hurts**. It's torture for your mind and your soul. Most of the time when you won't forgive someone for an offense, it is because you are holding them to a higher standard than you hold yourself to. In the words of Romans 2:1, "You may think you can condemn such people, but you are just as bad, and you have no excuse! When you say they are wicked and should be punished, you are condemning yourself, for you who judge others do these very same things."

Judging someone else's weaknesses without taking a long, hard look at your own is insanity. "Why worry about a speck in your friend's eye when you have a log in your own? How can you think of saying, 'Friend, let me help you get rid of that speck in your eye,' when you can't see past the log in your own eye? Hypocrite! First get rid of the log in your own eye; then you will see well enough to deal with the speck in your friend's eye" (Luke 6:41-42). So when someone, including your significant other, admits a wrong, you need to forgive them—for your own good as much as theirs. Release whatever they did, and let go of the Cupidity that's making your life a mess.

Forgiveness is not the same thing as accepting someone's sin. Love is to be unconditional, and so is our intolerance of sin. You unconditionally cannot accept sin into your life. When you allow sin to control you, you lose—even if it's the sin of the one you love.

Let's take a look at forgiveness—when it is required and when it isn't. First of all, let's establish that there are two healthy reactions to being harmed by another: forgiveness and getting over it. They are very similar but not exactly the same. According to Scripture, forgiveness is given to those who are truly sorry for their sin and repent, or turn away from it. "If another believer sins, rebuke that person; then if there is repentance, forgive" (Luke 17:3). A sense of remorse or regret always has to come before forgiveness, even when it comes to our relationship with God. "If we *confess* our sins to him, he is faithful and just to forgive us our sins and to cleanse us from all wickedness" (1 John 1:9, emphasis added).

Practically, to forgive is to agree with the offender that they sinned but to promise that you won't use it against them, bring it up again, or tell others about it. It means setting them free. That's why God requires repentance before forgiveness—an unrepentant soul cannot be set free from the punishment for sin (Luke 5:32; Acts 3:19). Repentance, according to Scripture, proves our sorrow for our sin, and because of that, forgiveness is required. "The kind of sorrow God wants us to experience leads us away from sin and results in salvation. There's no regret for that kind of sorrow. But worldly sorrow, which lacks repentance, results in spiritual death" (2 Corinthians 7:10).

Because of this requirement for forgiveness, we are not saying that a woman in an abusive relationship has to forgive the husband who continues to abuse her; that would be tolerating his sin. She must still learn to move beyond the offense; otherwise, she will remain his victim forever. But if the abusive husband repents of his ways and begs her for forgiveness, she must forgive him, according to God's Word.

A lot of people claim, "I'm just not as good as God" or "I'll let God forgive them." But when you say things like that, you're actually saying that your moral code is more rigorous than God's, because he can forgive a certain offense while you evidently can't (1 John 1:9). When you can't forgive, you disobey God's command to "be kind to each other, tenderhearted, forgiving one another, just as God through Christ has forgiven you" (Ephesians 4:32). When God takes your confession and hands you back forgiveness, he shows you how it's done. Saying, "That just doesn't work for me" is a total rejection of God's ways.

A lot of times when we're hurt, however, it isn't because of sin but because of an offense. When you are offended by someone else, it can feel like an attack. But every time you are having trouble getting over something, you have to ask yourself, *Was what they did a sin, or did they just hurt me?* Because last time we checked, **hurting you isn't a sin in itself**. Sure, the person might not have acted in what you perceive as love, or even kindness, but there is the distinct possibility that you didn't either. Often, especially in love relationships, we hear things that aren't even said. We misread or read between the lines and project our own emotions and thought patterns onto the other person. This is complete Cupidity.

When you make assumptions about people's motives, you are actually operating in deceit. You lie to yourself if you believe that your beloved, someone of the opposite sex, wants the same things you want and thinks the same way you think. That is why it is important to slow down and ask yourself about your grudge or inability to get over something your loved one has done. At any point that you can't forgive or get over something, you first have to ask yourself, *Am I unable to forgive a sin they have committed against me, or am I unable to let go of the pain they have caused me?* If your answer is in the affirmative, it reveals that your focus is inward instead of upward. If someone has offended you but not sinned against you, there is really nothing to forgive, since the only thing that needs to be forgiven is sin. Therefore it's just a question of, **can you get over it?** If you can't, then you are the one causing the pain in your life and in your relationship. You can't blame it on the other person's action because their action is over; it's your thought pattern that makes it continue. After all, it isn't what happens to you that hurts you but what you think about what happens to you that messes with your mind and emotions. (Except, of course, in the case of actual physical pain or abuse. For more on that, see #25.)

In all other situations, you have the power to get over things, to move on and change the atmosphere in your home, no matter what's going on. But it will take a reassigning of your hope. If you keep it all wrapped up in the other person, then you're going to be disappointed. But if your hope is wrapped up in a more godly direction, then you're sure to keep a strong footing. The easiest path isn't always the best one, and choosing to get over something is definitely the hard path. But it is also the most beneficial. After all, "If you forgive those who sin against you, your heavenly Father will forgive you. But if you refuse to forgive others, your Father will not forgive your sins" (Matthew 6:14-15). Clearly, when we look at forgiveness in light of this Scripture, it is for our own good. Refusing to forgive not only tortures us mentally but has an enormous impact on our relationship with God.

Getting over it is necessary in dealing with both the sins and the offenses that are committed against us. Jesus instructed us, "Love your enemies! Pray for those who persecute you!" (Matthew 5:44). And that is part of getting over it: learning to love the offender the way God does. Sin is to be confronted and rebuked, but non-sin offenses are things we just have to get over. In 1 Peter 2:23 we are told, "He did not retaliate when he was insulted, nor threaten revenge when he suffered. He left his case in the hands of God, who always judges fairly." Our reaction to attacks from others should always be the same position of humility taken by Christ. We can't make the person's sin or offense more important to us than God's Word, so we make it our goal not to be easily offended and to get over things quickly. And when forgiveness is asked for, we *give it freely*. Even if the person hurts us every day and asks us to forgive them every day, we keep on forgiving. Seventy times seven.

When you can't get over something or are unwilling to forgive, you are allowing sin to overwhelm and overtake your life. If you want freedom from this form of Cupidity, the best place to start is to forgive what needs to be forgiven and get over all the rest. There is more at stake than the culpability of another . . . and that is your very soul.

Forgivable Sins*

lying
cheating
stealing
anger
rebellion
discontentment
lack of self-control
bitterness
hatred
gossip
envy
drunkenness

Note: Everything on this list is still a sin.

Get-Over-Able Offenses**

disagreement
messiness
talking too much
not talking enough
bad cooking
not being into you (i.e., breaking up with you)
low wages
not mowing the lawn
not doing the dishes
not making the bed
washing a red towel with white shorts
not taking good care of your tools

**Note: Nothing on this list is a sin. Some things
might be incredibly annoying, yes, but sin, no.*

Emotions

5

Letting the Other Person's Emotions Control You

When someone you love is angry or depressed, it's hard not to let that affect you. A lot of arguments start when one person is uptight and they "share the love" with their significant other, and suddenly everyone is upset. It's not a pleasant gift, but there is a way to refuse the package: by not allowing their emotions to become your emotions. Sometimes people just feel upset or angry, and no matter what you do, you can't help them through it. But one thing is for sure: to join in their madness is madness.

We should never commiserate with others in their sinful emotions. Commiseration just makes for two miserable people, and it only fuels the fire of sin. It might feel like empathy, but empathy is only intended for godly feelings like sorrow, repentance, and long-suffering. The path of least Cupidity is to allow them their negative emotions, listen to how they're feeling, and then let it go, rather than to vicariously take it on as your own emotion. **Holding on to their anger and making it your own only makes matters worse.** When you choose joy and love and refuse to join in their emotions, you pour water on half of the fuel of the tension. And that helps things move toward reconciliation a lot more quickly. The world is angry enough as it is; more anger is not going to make things better. That's just counterintuitive.

The best way to keep good boundaries in this area is to refuse to take their anger as an attack on you personally whenever possible. Their anger is their anger, and while you must confess your part in it if you did something to lead them to anger, you don't have to defend yourself, because your job is understanding, not self-protection. It goes back to that classic image of light and darkness. If someone is in the dark, they don't want to be told it's not dark or it's not as dark as they think it is. Instead, show them empathy by acknowledging the darkness they're in and let them know you're there for them if they need anything. And then *you* *live in the light*. Let them see how much better it is to live that way so they can come out and join you (Ephesians 5:8-9). Don't teach them how by giving instructions; simply be a model citizen of the light. When we live rightly, others notice and want to join alongside us. And if you think about it, that's a much more effective way of breaking someone's funk than lecturing them or giving them a detailed instruction manual on how to proceed.

Emotional acts of Cupidity can strike us all at some point. Emotion can be a powerful blinder and an evil taskmaster. Even if you claim to be an unemotional person, chances are you still make some decisions based on your fear of emotions. So either way, emotional Cupidity is a relationally destructive force.

If you are prone to acts of emotional Cupidity, it might be time to take a look at where you are getting your emotional fuel—your emotional facts, if you will. Because anything you feel has a basis in your beliefs. If you believe that housewives are desperate or that sex should be a part of your city or that women should dress like NFL cheerleaders, maybe you've got some outside influences that are setting themselves up as universal truth when they are really just universal make-believe.

God's Word should be the only standard you use to measure love and your relationship. As soon as you let the world tell you how love should look, you lose. Because the world's vision of love takes a crew of hundreds. Makeup artists, stylists, cameramen, and script mavens all make love look the way they want it to look. But at home, without all the lights and the retakes and central casting, love looks a lot different. **Emotional Cupidity hurts.** It hurts not only you but also the ones you shoot with your little arrows. So before you take your next shot, consider where you are lying to yourself and how you can find out the truth.

Mental (Gender-Specific) Acts of Cupidity

Believing love is a feeling | Believing romance equals love | Standing on your rights | Misunderstanding forgiveness (or refusing to get over it) Letting the other person's emotions control you | Thinking that telling him everything is a good idea | Trying to fix things | Taking charge Failing to provide | Fearing the silence Refusing to grow up | Failing to notice him | Neglecting romance | Loving who you want him to become instead of who he is | Loving who she was instead of who she is | Not accepting his "kills" | Walking on eggshells | Refusing to receive protection or correction | Using sex to get love | Using romance to get sex | Believing sex will keep them | Withholding sex to get romance | Becoming too comfortable with each other Shacking up | Enabling abuse Having friends with benefits Blending finances before marriage Giving up food to get love

Loving her for her body only | Dressing to get attention | Looking at porn Having friends of the opposite sex Giving too much information Refusing to move forward emotionally Letting technology define your relationship | Pleasing the other person at all costs | Disrespecting your significant other in public | Refusing to apologize | Not knowing how to break up | Making a big deal out of everything Having unrealistic expectations Wishing your significant other were your gender Loving someone with a different faith | Expecting another person to bring you hope, joy, or peace Playing god | Obsessing over yourself | Obsessing over them | Rehearsing the other person's faults in your mind Sharing sins Not knowing what true love is

Mental (Gender-Specific) Acts of Cupidity 💜

Now that we've established that emotional acts of Cupidity can make you an emotional and relational wreck, we're required by law to let you know that your emotions might not be the only thing messing with your love life. Mental acts of Cupidity can make you seem crazy, especially to the opposite sex, but they can also cause your thinking to go crazy. Remember that emotional acts of Cupidity are the stupid things we do for love based on an emotion, such as fear or loneliness. Closely related but different (like a crazy uncle), mental acts of Cupidity usually have little to do with our emotions but instead are caused by unawareness. We make wrong assumptions about the opposite sex, or we just don't stop to think about what we're doing.

Mental Cupidity can come from a variety of sources: being taught misinformation by our parents and teachers, accepting inaccurate cultural norms, or allowing our minds to just get lazy. Regardless, we need to acknowledge the existence of these thought patterns so we can start the journey toward retraining that relational muscle memory. Mental acts of Cupidity might seem harmless enough since they're confined to your mind; after all, they aren't hurting anybody but you, so what's the big deal? But **your mind isn't an island**. It doesn't think in isolation. The people you have relationships with experience your mental acts of Cupidity as real as rain.

It's like this: you think about a thing so much that you can no longer resist taking some kind of action based on that thought.

And if the thought is total foolishness, you're in for some relational drama. The fact that everyone first thinks a certain way before acting that way (James 1:14-15) seems obvious, but then again so does using your blinker before making a turn.

Overcoming the Cupidity of the mind is a difficult challenge for all of us. Mental Cupidity can be like living in a trance, under the spell of so much stupid that you can't see straight. But therein lies the beauty of words on a page: somehow words have the ability to break into the Alcatraz of your mind and set you free to see the truth. Not that we have the answers to all of life's predicaments, but if there is anything that can break the cycle of Cupidity, it is getting a strong dose of truth. Cupidity finds nourishment when it's grown in ignorant bliss. When you have no idea that your thoughts about love are responsible for getting you into bad relationships or messing up the one you have, you stand no chance of breaking out and finding the freedom that could be yours—the freedom to love and be loved.

Mental acts of Cupidity are essentially the things you think about love that are in no way true. And as a friend of ours likes to say, **a half-truth is a whole lie**. Over time you've created your own kind of Cupid bible—the "truth" according to your love history or your life history. This canon is based on experiences from past relationships, what you've told yourself about how things should be, and promises you've made about things that should never ever happen again! Sometimes these thought patterns reflect God's Word and contain good stuff, but sometimes they're just plain Cupidity. Like when a person believes that nothing they do is ever wrong and every failed relationship has ended because of the other person. A man who has been divorced five times blames his inability to stay married on his bad luck and bad women. Or the

And Now a Brief Message
from a Sponsor of
Happiness

It may be said that it is the goal of every human being to be
HAPPY. Even for those who have never found it, happiness seems
to be at the core of all our searching. So let's dive into a little study
of happy—what makes you and your significant other happy, and
how you can provide that for each other. When two people take
their eyes off their own happiness and put it onto the happiness of
the other, everyone is covered. *Trouble happens when we focus
on our own happiness instead of that of those we love.* Another
word for it is selfishness, and it's a mental act of Cupidity.

Focusing on your own well-being or pleasure might seem like
the best way to get what you want, but in the end it gives you the
opposite of what you want. And it most often leads to bitterness,
frustration, and loneliness. Selfishness is never the healthy choice.
"Don't be selfish; don't try to impress others. Be humble, thinking
of others as better than yourselves. Don't look out only for your own
interests, but take an interest in others, too" *(Philippians 2:3-4)*.

Almost all acts of mental foolishness come from one source:
selfishness. It's understandable, since that is the natural state for human beings. We spend our whole lives keenly aware of what we are
feeling, wanting, needing, and thinking, so it takes a conscious effort
to get outside ourselves and into the hearts of others. Selfishness
promises self-protection and fulfillment, but that tendency can be
channeled in another direction when we transfer our need for protection and provision over to God. That frees us up to be concerned
about the happiness of others. Not that happiness is the ultimate
goal of life, but our willful, mental choice for our loved ones should
be their ultimate happiness rather than pain and torture. *So for this
discussion of romantic love, we will be majoring in the
happiness of others instead of the value of suffering and trials.*
Just to get that out on the table. ♥

woman who has never been asked on a second date says, "There are just no good men out there." But to that we say: there is one common denominator in each relationship that failed, and that's you. When you believe a lie about your relationship and that lie pushes you to act, you commit a mental act of Cupidity.

Misunderstanding the Man or Woman in Your Life

Most mental Cupidity is born out of a bellyful of ignorance. You don't intend on it; it just happens because you don't know any better or you haven't thought about it. Or maybe you do know better—you've simply sacrificed the spot in your brain that used to hold that information and given it over to something else. Either way, a little education on what makes men and women happy would do all of us some good.

There are a lot of things about men that women just don't get, and vice versa. Even after a truth about the opposite gender has been explained, there can be a lot of kickback. People say things like, "Well, that's stupid—why would they need that?" or "How ridiculous—I'm not going to do that." It's easy for both sexes to look at the desires of the other and assume they're completely broken. Why? Because those desires are often utterly different from their own. It's a funny thing, but God didn't make it so that men and women would want the exact same things in a relationship. And knowing God, he did that for a reason.

Although the roles of men and women, and even their desires, seem to conflict with each other, it can't go unnoticed that God designed them to complement one another. When God first created man and woman, he made woman the bringer of life, the nurturer who would give birth to humanity. And that role would require a provider—one who wasn't growing and caring for children but could go out and work the land, subdue it, kill the beasts, and provide shelter and protection for his family. Though today women can, and do, provide for and protect themselves, this need is still at the heart of their search for a man. The modern woman wants to feel safe when she is with a man, and she has a certain desire for him to be able to provide, should the need arise. It's no coincidence that in our marriage Hayley is the more obsessive one about setting the house alarm when Michael is out of town.

Her needs and his abilities; her abilities and his needs . . . all created in perfect union. So somewhere way back in the history of humanity, there was a reason for the differences that are still so obvious today. Whenever we complain about the strange desires of the opposite sex, we should *stop and consider the mastermind behind the whole situation* and note that he doesn't do anything stupid or useless. It's all there for some greater good.

So the first place to start is by accepting that men and women have different desires and wirings, and out of those come different needs in a relationship. If you haven't been factoring in these differences enough up to now, that could be a big reason for bumps in your current relationship (or lack thereof). This refresher course on the opposite sex might just be the kick in the pants you need to knock the Cupidity right out of you. So brace yourself, because here comes the foot.

Thinking That Telling Him Everything Is a Good Idea

Okay, so let's look at what makes a man happy. It's simple, really. One big thing that makes a man happy is when his woman is happy. Men don't always get things right in this pursuit, but if a man is (or ever has been) in love with a woman, then she can be sure that her happiness really is his desired outcome, no matter how bad he is at it. But a lot of times a woman's happiness is more dependent on her own mental state than on his actions. If a woman misunderstands her needs versus her wants or if she is ignorant about what makes a man happy, she can easily come across as unsatisfied, bitter, and desperately unhappy. And so she ignorantly spreads the wealth of negative emotions with her one true love.

When a man first falls for a woman, he will go to great lengths to give her what she wants. So he talks with her, romances her, buys her things, and does whatever he can to please her. He wants her to be happy. And when he succeeds, it makes him happy. Pretty simple. **He sees her happy; he's happy.** But women have a deep desire to communicate . . . everything! They want to share all their feelings, their deepest desires, and their innermost thoughts. And in the beginning that makes for a good pair. He wants her to be happy, so he listens. After he has heard what she craves, he tries to provide it in order to make her happy. Sometimes he's spot on, and other times he's way off. It's the wrong size, wrong color, wrong style, wrong taste, wrong thing to say, wrong emotion, or just not insightful enough.

And the woman, in her desire to communicate her deepest emotions, tells him exactly how she feels about his gift or his effort. Because the woman has reverse-engineered all this to say, "Well, if I'm not truly happy, then he's not going to be happy either, so I'm going to tell him everything that isn't perfect in my life!" But if all a man hears is how everything is not perfect, he thinks he has failed, because the absence of perfection means that his woman could be happier. And *with each "not happy," he is knocked down*. It is mental Cupidity for a woman to be unaware that telling a man exactly what she is thinking without regard for how it will make him feel beats him down and makes her seem ungrateful and high maintenance.

The remedy to this problem is a simple one but one of the most difficult from a muscle memory standpoint: shut up. Shut up and stay out of trouble. Or put more nicely, "Watch your tongue and keep your mouth shut, and you will stay out of trouble" (Proverbs 21:23). If a woman is telling a man something just to get it off her chest, to make herself feel better, or to break down on a scale of one to ten why his gift or his effort was an eight, then she should reconsider whether it needs to be said. When a woman expresses her negative emotions about what a man has done for her or even about things that have nothing to do with him, he often takes it as a personal assessment of his ability to make her happy. There might be nothing further from the truth, but it is selfish and careless for her to assume his heart will take something exactly as she meant it. Living outside of ourselves means understanding how others process information as it comes out of our mouths. When we place our desires for self-expression above the feelings of the other person, love suffers.

For example, a smart woman of old would run out to the man who brought home a big antelope for dinner and hug his neck, saying, "Thank you, thank you, thank you! I can't wait to prepare this for our family." But now men bring home things like new garbage cans, bath mats, lawn furniture, and vehicles. And it's easy to say, "Oh, I hate that color." Or he takes her on a date to a new restaurant, and she complains about the bad food and poor service the rest of the night. It seems harmless enough. It's the truth, and it's not a direct attack on him . . . oh, but to his heart it is. He might not ever tell this to the woman he loves, but the moment she condemns what he has done for her, he gives up a bit of his passion and desire to please her. When pleasing her seems almost an impossibility, he has a hard time making the effort again. Contrast that to when a man fulfills a woman's needs and she appreciates his skills. With her simple expression of gratitude, she delivers *a huge dose of love to her man* and builds his strength better than any protein shake.

One of the biggest problems a woman tends to have in a relationship with a man is thinking that talking pleases him as much as it pleases her. Women often forget the proverb that says, "Those who control their tongue will have a long life; opening your mouth can ruin everything" (Proverbs 13:3). A woman who dumps on her man, who believes that if she is feeling it he should have to hear about it, lies to herself and hurts the very relationship she innately wants to nurture.

She can't understand why at the end of a long day he doesn't want to sit down and talk with her or, uh, listen to her. He's tired. And after working a hard day, he needs rest in order to be refreshed and ready for the next day. But most women who work hard all day don't see rest and relaxation as an option. At the end of a long day they feel their duties still aren't done. They see a house that needs more work, and they get to it. They want to tell the men in their lives everything that needs to be fixed and everything that went wrong so the man can get on board and help out. But that isn't how a man operates. There is nothing wrong with him; he's just designed differently.

Do everything without complaining. PHILIPPIANS 2:14

He's wired to shut down after a long day of work, while she's wired to keep on going. The smart woman accepts her man the way he is and gives him some time to wind down before she dumps on him. Or she doesn't dump at all, but wisely picks her opportunities to talk to him about something important or ask him for help.

Men want to feel needed. And when a woman has a problem, her best bet is to bring it to her man with the intent of asking for his help. If she just wants to dump, then she needs to keep in mind that dumping isn't a normal occurrence in the life of a man. For the most part, a man goes to another man with a problem only when he wants his help, not just to get it off of his chest. Women are wired differently, and they get a huge sense of relief when they can just talk about it and get it out there, even if the problem doesn't get fixed. Once most men are made aware of a problem and have involved themselves in the problem, they typically won't stop until it's solved.

To the Dump, *to the Dump,*
to the Dump, Dump, Dump

Some things should be saved for girlfriends who are geared to listen to venting without taking it personally. A man can't listen to the woman he loves complain, without feeling responsible for her state of unhappiness, so when a woman just wants to dump, she'd be showing love to her man if she finds a girlfriend, instead of him, to go to the dump with.

Here are a few things that won't make his life any better to know:

- ✦ *her latest personal grooming disasters*
- ✦ *her friend's unruly child*
- ✦ *her weight problem*
- ✦ *her bad hair day*
- ✦ *her lack of anything to wear*
- ✦ *her annoying coworker*
- ✦ *her messy house*
- ✦ *her PMS (unless it's like a storm alert)*

It is Cupidity to think that a man should accept a woman's dumpage and react counter to his wiring. He basically sees it as *a honey-do list to her happiness*. So the next time she wants to dump, she should load up the truck, drive it over to a friend's house, unload it on her living room floor, and sift through it with her—including all the dirty dishes, socks, stinky food, and other remnants of her life. Another female will understand that it's only an exercise of lifting the heavy load and that her friend doesn't really want her to help clean up the mess.

If a woman really wants to talk with her husband/significant other, or she has no other option, she can at the very least set up the conversation. She can ask him if he has five minutes to listen to her and tell him she doesn't need his advice and doesn't want him to fix it (unless she does); she just needs to talk. Then he'll be prepared for her dumpage. He has been set up, and he's much less likely to say something "wrong" or to take something the wrong way.

Trying to Fix Things

When a man talks to another man about a problem, it means he wants help fixing it. A man usually tries to fix things himself and brings up an issue only if he really feels incapable of doing it himself and could use a little direction. So when a woman starts talking about her problems, a man takes that as an indication that he is being asked to fix things—to *do* something. But when a woman talks, it is usually not her goal to be "fixed." Her goal is to be heard and sympathized with. This can seem like a waste of time and energy to the average man. Okay, even to the above-average man. But that's where the everyman is going to have to become more strategic and less reactive. He needs to learn to listen with discipline!

When a woman talks about her problems, all she usually wants is for him to be attentive and to look sad when she is sad and stressed when she is stressed. She wants him to agree with her and understand her. As she talks all around a subject, weaving in and out of ideas, maybe even not making sense to the man listening, she feels a release, and amazingly, a connection. The longer a man listens, the more connected she feels. A man can't let this mystery derail him from what might seem to him a waste of time. Listening to her—giving her that time to be heard—is more of a gift than he could ever imagine. That means he can't take on her problems as his problems or as an indictment of him. Her fears and worries aren't accusations, only outlets for her emotional life. If a man can listen without feeling the pain of condemnation or powerlessness, he has learned to love well. And he has provided for her emotionally.

Of course, this call to listen doesn't mandate the removal of a man's brain cells or his spiritual and manly sensibilities. While many problems can be listened to, some need to be addressed as spiritual or emotional danger zones that only someone who is legally bound to love her would be brave enough to correct. In our relationship, we look at each other as **God's tools of sanctification**. If one of us sees in the other a spiritual dark spot, an area blinded by emotions or negative thought patterns, we are committed to fearlessly call each other on it (Colossians 1:28; 2 Timothy 3:16-17; 4:2). We have also agreed to be emotionally receptive when we are on the receiving end. Many people—men and women—buck at the strain of spiritual investigation into their lives and consider correction heartless and emotionally intrusive, but that should never stop us from intervening when we need to. We just have to be really diligent in doing what the Bible commands us to do, and that is to speak the truth *in love*, gently and humbly (Galatians 6:1; Ephesians 4:15).

Taking Charge

Men thrive on accomplishment. They are most happy when they can say, "See what I did." When a man is pursuing a woman, his accomplishment comes as he chases her and ultimately catches her. The harder she is to get, the more successful he's going to feel when he gets her. His sense of value at having been strong enough, good enough, man enough to land the woman he worked so hard to get is strengthened in the getting. That's the reason we encourage women to be mysterious . . . to let the man chase, to let him enjoy everything that goes along with that.

When single women refuse to be chased and instead turn the tables and do the pursuing themselves, it's like playing tag with someone who, in the middle of the game, turns around and starts running after the guy who is "it." It takes away the challenge and the fun. And usually the guy who's "it" will start running away! If a single woman wants to make a man happy, she will refuse to chase him and let him do the chasing himself. **Easy has never been a compliment unless you're an office supply store selling red "easy" buttons.**

The struggle for control dates back to the Garden of Eden, when God "gifted" both sexes with the consequences for the sins of the first man and woman. And he did it masterfully. Knowing both of his kids so well, he gave each of them the punishment that would most impact them. Just like parents do today, God took away from each something they loved and made each do something they hated. From Eve, he took her ability to lead alongside her man, to control things—something she clearly wanted. And God gave her something she most definitely didn't want, and that was increased pain in childbirth (Genesis 3:16). Speaking from the experience of forty hours of labor and an emergency C-section, thanks, Eve! From Adam, God took his ability to have it easy; read: "be lazy" (Genesis 3:17). The Garden was a pretty good gig. Tend the garden, pick the fruit, name the animals, play with God. Now all of a sudden Adam was dealing with his punishment: backbreaking work! What a deal. That was taking away something Adam must have loved—the easy life. But later Adam was given something else that didn't come naturally, and that was the command to love his wife in spite of her newfound flaws. Notice that God didn't command the wife to love her husband, perhaps because love comes naturally to a woman. But *she is commanded to do what doesn't come naturally*: respect her husband (Ephesians 5:33).

There is a natural desire inside all women to be in control. That should come as no shock to any of us. God's Word confirms it: "You will desire to control your husband" (Genesis 3:16). The thing is, when a modern woman is single, she has to control her own life, her own destiny, and no one is responsible for getting things done except her. Back in the day that wasn't so. Women lived under the authority and protection of their fathers until the time they married, and then they lived under the authority and protection of their husbands. Yet still there was a battle for control. So imagine how much more difficult things are now, when women are independent for years before getting married and have been forced to be in control of everything. It shouldn't be a shocker that when a woman marries a man whose call is to be the leader, there is friction. Any time a woman attempts to gain back what was taken away from Eve, she's in for a fight.

A controlling woman never makes a man happy. No man is content to be led around by a female, no matter how much she thinks he is. If he isn't complaining, it's either because he's too afraid to (emotional act of Cupidity) or he doesn't know any better (mental act of Cupidity). Though the woman may feel at the top of her game doing what needs to be done, when she takes control away from her man, she disrespects him. And disrespect has two outcomes: One is that it can make her man weak, like a pet goldfish that hasn't been fed for a week. Pretty soon he'll be floating at the top of the bowl. You've seen this on the glazed-over faces of men staring at the TV while their wives yell in their ears, believing that the louder they yell, the more likely their husbands will be to hear and get moving.

And two, when a woman takes over something, anything, a man can easily assume his natural stance—the path of least resistance—and give up doing that particular thing forever. So if a woman starts asking a guy out and planning everywhere they go, she'll be doing it for the rest of the relationship. Guys are simple creatures, easily taught by deeds if not words. If a woman shows a man that she will do something, he'll more than likely just let her keep on doing it so he doesn't have to fight her. Of course, there are some men who react differently to being devalued. These men feel disrespect and return the favor. If a woman feels unloved and unappreciated by her man, she might look at her own heart and see if she has any disrespect lingering there for him.

Bossy, nagging, unthankful, difficult, a dripping faucet . . . these are just a few descriptions given to a woman who tries to be, well, the boss. It's just not sexy. It's not appealing when a woman tells a man what to do. She can make him happy, and get happy herself, by letting go and letting the guy be the guy . . . by taking on some responsibility. If she's having trouble, she might want to ask herself if it's because she doesn't trust him. Or is it because she doesn't trust God to speak to him, to work out everything for good? Much of disrespect comes from distrust. A woman distrusts a man's choices because she fears they might lead to disaster. She doesn't believe he will do things right. For most women, distrust and disrespect really are **classic signs of pride**: "No one can do it better than I." But that betrays a heart of doubt, not a heart of faith. When a woman has faith in God and therefore faith that things will work out, even if she isn't the one in charge, she is very appealing to her man.

Of course the single woman can't turn her life over to the man she is dating—that in itself would be an act of Cupidity since she isn't married to him. But she can begin to let go and stop controlling their dating relationship by making demands, asking too many questions, and constantly wanting real-time status updates on defining the relationship. All those behaviors are ultimately acts of disrespect. A woman in a dating relationship should allow the man to exercise his leadership muscles and experience what it is like to lead her as a woman.

Cupidity for the married woman is refusing to respect her man because of who he is and what he has done. Respect isn't totally

Letting Him Lead While Dating

Practically speaking, here are some ways a single woman can learn to let the man lead, as well as show him how well she follows.

Let him plan and pay for dates. When a woman takes over this responsibility, she is teaching him to follow her lead, and that sets a precedent for the future of the relationship.

Let him control the speed of the relationship. In other words, a woman should let him move the relationship along at a healthy pace, unless of course his pace is bullet train speed; then she can tap the brakes and just follow him at a slower pace than he is going. If he's a good guy, he'll slow down and wait for her. If not, he wasn't meant for her anyway.

Let him get the door. It sounds like a little thing, but when a woman rushes to open the door for herself, she takes away something that he could do for her. So a woman would do well to just slow down as she approaches a door and let him open it for her. It's hard to follow when you are the one in front. Could this be a good analogy for the spiritual life? Hmmm, just a thought.

unconditional, like real love is, but it should be close, with only the most heinous acts giving her pause. A woman doesn't expect her husband to stop loving her when she upsets him or even hurts him, so she shouldn't live with the double standard that her respect is conditional on his actions.

For example, consider a woman who says, "I can't respect my

husband—he's too angry and speaks harshly to me all the time" or "How can I respect a man who has been out of work so long?" On paper the answer might very well be that she can't respect someone like that. But God's Word doesn't make exceptions when it comes to respect. We aren't commanded to respect our parents only as long as they are good to us (Ephesians 6:1-2), nor does God command women to respect only good or wealthy husbands (Ephesians 5:33). A husband deserves respect based on the role and responsibility God has given him, not whether he has "proved" himself worthy.

The crux of the matter is that **another's sin is never an excuse for ours**—two wrongs don't make a right. But

When Women Take Charge of the Relationship

By nature, men are professional relaxers. They don't look for things to do; they try to find ways to rest. So when the woman takes over, he usually lets her, and it goes something like this:

She wants to go on a date, so she calls him, makes the plans, picks him up, and pays. Phew! Now he doesn't have to do anything but wait for her to call, plan, and pay again.

She wants the lawn mowed, so she just does it. He never mows again.

She sees him not providing enough financially, so she gets a job. She makes more than he does anyway, so why should he work?

when a woman acts rightly in the face of mistreatment or dis-respect, she honors the God who promised to love those who obey his Word, no matter the circumstances (John 15:10; James 1:2-4; 1 John 5:2). Respect is conditional only on a woman's choice to obey God's Word. If she chooses to obey, then she must respect her husband. Of course, for the single woman, this command doesn't apply. She is not required to respect a man she is not married to. And that means that if he is angry, unkind, out of work, or anything else that mars her respect for him, she doesn't have to accept him as the one for her. She can look at those red flags and say good-bye while good-bye can still be said.

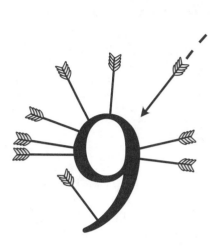

Failing to Provide

Historically, men have been the providers in relationships. Grog went out and killed the beast and brought it back home for his woman. Jeb went out into the field and tilled the soil to bring back the harvest for his wife. For eons it has been the man who has provided for his woman. In the days way before Olive Garden and grocery stores and bimonthly paychecks, the man provided by killing things with sharp knives and dragging them back home for the family to devour. He served his purpose; he protected and provided for the woman he loved. And this provision made him invaluable to her.

Provision doesn't just start and end with money. There are other ways men can provide for women without getting financial. Emotional provision is also a big need for women. Maybe it's a symptom of our overworked society or urban sprawl or our addiction to material goods, but whatever it is, women the world over are noticing how hard it is to find and make friends. The need that women have for emotional support and nurture, then, is falling more heavily on their men. Back in the

ARE YOU **MAN** ENOUGH?

In the dating rituals of the 1940s and 1950s, the man was expected to ask, plan, pick up, and pay. Trust us, there was a day when that was the norm. If a guy took a girl to the soda shop and asked her to go dutch, he could be sure he'd never see her again. Provision tells a woman that a man cares and that she's worth it. And more than that, it tells her that he is man enough to provide for her. Even though nowadays many women make more money than men, there is still something embedded in the DNA that makes both sexes feel like everything is well when the man pays and the woman enjoys. Could it be written on the woman's soul, this need for provision? After all, the biblical role of the male as leader and lover could easily be said to include the act of providing for the loved one. God is a good example of this provision—as the ultimate leader and lover, he clearly provides for all our needs (Genesis 22:14; Psalm 111:5). And in Ephesians 5:28-29 and 1 Timothy 5:8, men are commanded to provide for their wives and families.

But what does provision mean anymore? How can he do for her what she can't do for herself when she clearly can do it all for herself? When a couple is dating, there is an obvious and easy solution. The man can ask her out, plan the date, pick her up, and pay. When he does that, he provides for her very clearly. This kind of provision lets the heart of a woman know not only that he cares emotionally but that he can provide for her physically. The trouble is that many women, because they have had to drive their own lives and make their own way in the corporate and financial worlds, have forgotten how to receive provision. And because of that some might balk at it. But balking isn't all bad, and it isn't permanent. Most women, especially Christian women, want a man who is a leader. They've read Scripture—they know how things are supposed to look and they know they want it—they just haven't had a lot of experience with it. It's a risk all right, but it's one worth taking.

days before the majority of women entered the workforce, their emotional needs were cared for primarily by other women who worked in the home next door or across the street. Women found time to talk, share, create, and nurture one another throughout the day, getting that part of their needs met by each other. But once they started leaving the home and going to work, women lost some of that vital connection with other women, leaving them vulnerable to emotional exhaustion. Couple that with the rugged individualism that has become the norm in our country, and you get women who are having a very hard time making friends.

With that turn of events, men are left with a larger bulk of the emotional provision. Men must learn to, at the end of their day, provide more emotional support for their wives and shoulder a significant load of the homemaking. Sure, a man can opt out of the emotional work, but the cleanup he'll have to do after her emotional meltdown will likely turn out to be more work than the initial investment ever would have been. While we would be the first to say it is the woman's job to reach out to other women and find the emotional connections she needs rather than expecting her husband to meet all her feminine needs, we also aren't going to tell men that they can get off so easy. In many cases, the man has to **step up to the plate** and share an emotional burden for his wife. But before the guys reading this pass out flat on the floor at the prospect, let's just say it's more strategy than heavy lifting.

Michael:

The Trouble with Provision,
PART 1 (THE GUY'S PART)

Hey, it's me—the one without the ovaries. When we were first engaged, it was super hard for Hayley to imagine giving that provision part of her life over to a man. She had her own car, her own home, and her own fledgling business. **She was independent and assertive.** But she had a strong desire to please God, so she worked through, though painfully, her desire to be in control and manage her own life. And I helped her by not allowing her to give up or be scared off. I took my biblical responsibilities to heart, and though I listened to her complaints on the subject, I didn't let those complaints steer the conversation (well, most of the time). It's part of being a man to know that even though a wife may argue, it doesn't make her right or more in control. It's hard for a man to see the love of his life angry or fearful, but when he loves God even more, he has the strength to walk her through this process in love. ♥

Hayley:

The Trouble with Provision,
PART 2 (THE WOMAN'S PART)

The funny part is that *I wanted more than anything to be provided for.* I'd dreamed of it; I'd even fantasized about it. I just didn't know how to live it out in my daily life. I consistently took and kept control in my relationships and continued to date guy after guy who couldn't *step up to the plate* and provide for me. Having a man who could take care of me and be a leader was pure romance in the figment of my dreams, but it didn't carry over into my daily life. Thank God for a man who didn't give in to my weakness but chose to walk on in obedience, no matter how much screaming he had to put up with for a time.

When a woman works outside of the home, most of her day is spent in a business environment, setting goals, managing, accomplishing, and reevaluating, so it can be hard for women to switch gears to be the gentle, loving partner most men would love to come home to. In fact, most women, truth be told, would love to come home to a spouse of their own who has the home, the food, and the kids all under control so she can pour herself into a nice hot bubble bath and unwind from another tough day.

So what is the solution? A man has to be determined to understand the challenges his wife faces and allow her time to transition. *Transition will usually entail talking.* She needs to talk about everything she has done and felt during the day in order to purge it. He may have exhaustion of his own that he deals with in the exact opposite way, but what she's looking for is someone to listen. Little to no talking is required of him; **we aren't suggesting that he become one of the girls**. He just needs to allow her to slip back into her feminine nature and leave work behind. Of course, we'd be remiss not to mention that most often a man has to resist the temptation to try to fix everything she's telling him about! (See #7.)

Beyond listening there must be a conscious effort to not let her continue in the same leadership pattern she functions in at work, because oftentimes that is a distinctly male pattern. She needs to be allowed to *fall back into her female role* so that the male/female dynamics can remain balanced in the home. If she doesn't bounce back to "bride," the tendency will be for her husband to take on the bride characteristics of the relationship. Not good—that's when things get really uncomfortable. A man must provide for his woman as a man, not by picking up the feminine slack.

Fearing the Silence

Another sour note in the music of romance is fearing his silence. When men have a rough day, when they have a problem, or when they are just worn out, most of them don't want to talk. And women, who typically like to talk when things get rough, often don't understand why the men in their lives are retreating and not communicating with them. It is easy for a woman to take a man's silence as an indictment of her or of their relationship. In the mind of a woman, the most obvious reason for silence is relational friction.

"What's wrong?" she asks, and he says, "Nothing" and walks off. Her immediate thought is, *What did I do?* If he's not willing to talk about it, she assumes it must be because he's mad at her. But that is mental Cupidity on her part. It's often not true, and it's projecting her own way of thinking and behaving onto him. In order to stop this flawed mentality in its tracks, women need to **stop fearing silence** and start understanding that men deal with stress and fatigue much differently than women do. They tend to work things out in the privacy of their own cave.

When a man comes home grumpy and out of sorts, what he

needs, usually, is to be alone, with nothing but a TV, a video game, or a project and some tools. This makes no sense to the woman he's in a relationship with, but that doesn't matter—it's what he needs to do to work through his stuff. When a woman lets him do that without trying to make him talk, he feels respected and able to unwind. And when that happens, he can rebound back to his normal self. But when the woman doesn't let him get the rest he needs, he feels resentful and angry. It is selfishness for a woman to begrudge the design of a man that causes him to need a different outlet for stress than she needs.

It's not just married women who need to understand this truth about men. Single women would do well to realize that *silence isn't death to the relationship*. If he doesn't call right after a date, it doesn't mean he isn't interested. If there are days of phone silence, it doesn't mean he has moved on. When a woman reads his silence like it's a book written start to finish, she starts to panic. And then she does all kinds of crazy things to get his attention, like calling him, asking him what's wrong, pursuing him. This eventually chases him off or wears him down—either way, it doesn't encourage his manliness or his leadership.

When a woman learns to allow for the silence, it is a gift of happiness to the man in her life. *Words aren't the cure for every problem* . . . sometimes they are the cause. In the pursuit of loving a man, a woman must give him what he needs, even if it's not always what she wants.

Interpreting "Man Silence"

If a woman finds herself stuck with a man who doesn't want to talk, here are some things she can consider before she goes off the deep end worrying about what she did or didn't do to make him this way.

End of the day silence: When a guy comes home, says, "Hey," and heads straight for his man-cave just after hugging the dog and throwing a tennis ball for his daughter to chase, it's important for the wife to remember it's not about her. Chances are he had a **rough day at work** and he needs some alone time to decompress. Men usually don't need or want to talk things out, so when she lets him have that time to manage the strain of his day in silence, it will help him recover more quickly. Even Jesus taught his disciples to rest and seek solitude after a hard day's work (Mark 6:31-32).

Early morning silence: Face it, not everyone is a morning person. And by and large, few men are talkative in the morning. That doesn't mean they aren't early risers; they just tend to be, well, silent risers. Usually this phenomenon taps into **the provision muscle**—men are silently working through the tasks and pitfalls they will need to negotiate in that dawning day. And since most men don't want to talk it out or talk it through, that leaves either silence, allowing him to get that mental preparation done, or small talk with his woman, leaving him with a distracted and stressed mind. We can't emphasize enough that, if possible, a man must beat his wife up every morning. Wait, before you do anything rash, that means he needs to rise and prepare in solitude before meeting his other half in conversation to connect their schedules, tasks, and hearts for the new day. It's worth noting that Jesus repeatedly rose at daybreak and went to a solitary place before meeting up with his disciples again (Mark 1:35; Luke 4:42).

Argument silence: Okay, this can go both ways (women can act like this too), but for the most part, men tend to go silent at certain points during heated conversations. There are a couple of reasons why this happens. One, if the guy starts feeling a tad enraged, he may be trying to implement the old axiom, "If you've got nothing nice to say, don't say anything at all." The worst thing a woman can do in this situation is to press him. All the amped-up emotions that he's trying to keep in check (a very gentlemanly thing to do, BTW) are just going to be super-charged if she keeps pressing him to "open up." Remember, most **guys like to process internally**. And this leads to the second point. Argument silence can also be a healthy mechanism for a guy to avoid getting in trouble. If he feels like a woman is too emotional, stressed, or whatever, a wise guy might find "none of the above" the best answer to an argument in the heat of the moment.

Driving silence: Have you ever heard of a race car driver having a long, involved conversation with his crew? Nope, he just drives, listens to his spotter, gives feedback on the car's performance when necessary, and tries to avoid putting his car into the wall. For a lot of guys, **driving is an allegory of their inner nature** and their love of the chase, so ladies, don't be ticked off when men are just making their turns and passing the competition.

Movie/TV silence: This one might sound silly, but we hear a lot of men ask the question, "Why do women want to talk during movies?" Maybe it's a woman's desire to experience the movie with her man, but usually a man wants to immerse himself in the movie as **a vehicle of escape**. And his date ain't in it! A common guy perspective is that movies are made to be watched and *then* talked about. So movie silence isn't about her; it's about him immersing himself in the experience. She'd be wise to save the questions until after the movie—he might be ready to download then.

Refusing to Grow Up

A lot of single women are looking around wondering where all the men are. They see lots of boys, but few men. Sure, if a guy is over twenty-one, he should consider himself a grown male, but if he refuses to grow up emotionally and is unable to lead, he brings the wrath of his immaturity onto the women who are stepping out, starting careers, and running businesses. Women today find themselves moving into adulthood much earlier than many of their male counterparts, and they resent that fact. Blame it on overprotective mothers, absentee fathers, or a failure to tackle hard things, but whatever the cause, when a guy does all he can not to grow up, he is living in Cupidity.

There are a lot of fears that go along with a guy's refusal to grow up, but probably the biggest is the **fear of responsibility**. It is responsibility that makes a man a man. And when he refuses it, he chooses boyhood as his perpetual state. Commitment to a woman, and all that goes along with it, can sound ominous and life changing (and not in a good way). But regardless of that perception, commitment and responsibility are needed so he can become the man he was meant to be. And while that might sound all "Hallmark" and like total inspirational fluffitude, check it out: Luke 16:10 says, **"If you are faithful in little things, you will be faithful in large ones."** Parents don't trust their little boy with the privileges of a young man until he has proven himself responsible. So why would God entrust him with a wife when he still acts like a little boy? A man isn't a kid; he *has* kids with his wife and grows them into adults. Start by making yourself into one first!

How to Know if You Are Stunting Your Growth

You are over twenty-one and you still live at home.

You can't keep a job for more than a few months.

You play video games for more than two hours a day. (Hayley says: "No insult to you, Michael—I know it's youth culture research." Michael says: "I can't believe she still buys that!")

On your last three dates, you went to restaurants with drive-throughs.

Your parents still pay your bills.

You have a subscription to *Maxim*, *FHM*, or *Highlights for Children*.

You've been dating a woman more than five years, and you haven't asked her to marry you.

You spend more time with your friends than with your girlfriend/wife.

Failing to Notice Him

One of the things that makes a man feel like he has arrived is when he has the admiration of a woman. His job—to provide and care for her—leads him to want admiration for getting the job done. Admiration, the verbalizing of her appreciation, means a lot to him. It makes him happy. And when he's happy, he's strong and able to do more of what makes *her* happy.

There are a lot of things a woman can admire about a man. She can admire anything about him that is distinctly male. When she recognizes his manliness and all that goes with that, it is a great compliment to him. So to make a man happy, a woman simply has to admire *his guy stuff*—his strength, his ability to make decisions and money, his emotional self-control, his problem solving, his big hands, his man skills, his manly features, his manly smell. Anything that says, "You are a man" is a compliment to him and makes him feel admired. Men don't want much—they just want the women in their lives to notice them for who they are and what they do.

Men are truly simple creatures, while women

tend to be more complicated and have trouble grasping a man's simplicity. Ask any car mechanic, and they'll tell you they'd much rather work on an old muscle car engine from the sixties than a computerized, fuel-injected hybrid of today. The reason? Simplicity and room to work under the hood. So if a woman wants to make a man happy, she'll just keep it simple: "You are so strong. I love your big hands and your strong back" or "You're so good with cars, computers, providing, etc." Simple words ... too simple? Some women will say yes—this is not deep enough; it is disrespectful in its simplicity. But nothing could be further from the truth. Women need to stop projecting their desires and needs onto the men they love. **He isn't a woman.**

Women might think this need for affirmation seems too childish: "You mean I have to tell you how good you are to make you happy? How silly." And to that, a man could easily say, "So when you ask me how you look in that dress, you don't want to hear that you look beautiful? You don't care if I say you look fat?" The central fallacy of mental Cupidity is believing that men and women want the same things and then acting on that belief. Stupid. Not bright. Whether or not admiration makes sense to the female mind is irrelevant. The fact that it makes him feel like king of the world is all that matters.

Michael:

Appreciation > Depreciation

I want to give Hayley props. Whenever we go out to dinner, Hayley always thanks me for paying. Even though it's her money too, she makes it a point to say thank you for picking

Seven Ways to Admire Him

— Tell him how well he did at taking care of something around the house.

— Compliment his abilities in front of his friends.

— Remind him how safe he makes you feel when you are out together.

— Thank him every time he does something for you.

— If he corrects you, don't argue to prove yourself right. Just say, "Thank you so much for caring."

— When he has a win in his life, congratulate him.

— Never make fun of his masculine tendencies— appreciate them.

the place, planning the date, and paying for it. Her admiration of my ability to provide for her makes me feel like I'm doing my job, and that makes me happy. It isn't much, but it's enough to put a smile on my face. And it's not just me. **Give any guy some appreciation, and you prove your love.**

But to be fair, while admiration has a great payoff to any woman in a relationship with a man, it is not a biblical mandate. It's just something guys want, and it encourages them to love better. But even if it's not a command, appreciation is a God-honoring idea. You might say it's a first cousin of the respect God commands women to have for their husbands. No matter how you look at it, it's a great practice for anyone who wants to make a man happy.

Neglecting Romance

For the majority of women in the Western world, romance is their number one goal in a relationship. But for a man, romance is only the frosting on the cake. A woman craves romance like a man craves admiration. She mourns the absence of it and becomes jealous over its existence anywhere other than in her life. She might not always be able to put it into words, but if she is like most women, ***romance is her love gauge***. And it goes like this: As a man provides romance for the woman in his life, she feels loved. As he neglects romance, she feels like the love is leaving. Her feelings are more than likely wrong—his love hasn't run off. He feels the same way about her today as he did when he was wining and dining her in the beginning of the relationship. So what's the big deal?

A man doesn't have to share—or even completely grasp—a woman's views of romance. But if he wants to make her happy, he might want to up the romance. Romance is not a biblical mandate. There is no eleventh commandment that says, "Romance the woman you love so that things will go well with you." But there could be a law of Cupidity that states, "When you forget the romance, she forgets the admiration." As a man romances a woman, she feels valued. And that sense of value translates as love to her feminine heart.

Seven Signs That a Guy Has Lost the Romance Race

+ She says things like, "You don't love me anymore!"
+ She buys flowers for herself on major holidays.
+ She complains that you love _____ more than her.
+ She watches a romantic comedy and can't stop crying.
+ She says romance is a waste of time.
+ She doesn't jump at the chance to be with you.
+ She has stopped saying little phrases of admiration.

There are women who would object to the idea of this feminine longing for romance. She claims she doesn't want it; in fact, she runs from it. But truth be told, somewhere along the way she determined that romance would never be hers. She was hurt, burned, abused, and the romance she craved as a little girl who dreamed of Prince Charming riding in on his white steed was strangled, suppressed, and swept under the rug of her heart. Now she objects to romance, but that is only because she has taken the role of the leader, of the man, in the relationship. **There is room for only one man and one woman in a relationship.** So if either of the sexes is filling the role of their counterpart, that leaves a vacuum. A woman who leads leaves a vacuum of femininity in her relationship that easily becomes filled by the man, and vice versa. Suddenly the roles become reversed. He's needy, wanting her time and attention. And she's busy, grumpy, and uninterested in the gentler aspects of life. When things get all topsy-turvy and the roles get reversed, nothing makes sense to anyone.

A change from this pattern can happen, but it requires work on the part of both people in the relationship. The woman needs to find a *desire to change*, and the man needs to find the strength to react more like a man and less like a girlfriend. That will allow her to take on the more feminine role and, as a result, the feminine needs.

For most women, a move back to romance will make them feel like they have ultimate importance in a man's life. It's hard for them to believe in a man's love when he spends most of his time working or golfing or doing stuff online. Most women translate a man's ability to give so much to his work or other activities and so much less at home as playing favorites. *After all,* she reasons, *he must favor work over me because he gives it more effort and time.* And effort doesn't just mean on your anniversary or on date night. Date night is effort, but most women would trade that for quantity time. But if a couple's financial situation rules out the ability to supply quantity, then quality effort it must be. A woman desperately wants to experience a man's efforts, not just his finances, expended on her behalf. And that can take many forms—such as when he takes the time to give her a massage for no reason at all. Or when he hugs her at every given opportunity. Or when he calls her during the day or brings home dinner. Whatever he can do that tells her he put forth an effort to make her life more comfortable, she will love him for it.

Now we know from conversations we've had with other couples that these attempts at romance aren't always received in love at first. Some women might reject them as interruptions in their busy day or as unwanted advances, and that could be because of the strain on their busy schedules or because of building resentment about some aspect of the relationship. Whatever the cause, a man can't let her rejection pass by unattended. For a man to lead, he has to refuse to go with the flow she creates in her tsunami of busyness. And he can't just accept the status quo, relinquishing control of the relationship to her broken past or bad muscle memory. That would be a failure to lead. But getting leadership back when it has been abdicated isn't an easy process. A man has to think on his feet in order to lead a woman rather than follow her, and he has to be fearless in giving love. That means that when he feels the rejection of his love, he has to gently call her on her failure to let him lead.

Leading a woman can be like shooting free throws, in the sense that repetition and consistency are the keys to making it work. And consistency takes time. Any basketball coach or pure shooter will tell you to use the same routine at the free throw line and keep your shot consistent, no matter the distractions from other players or the crowd. A man has to diligently reject her inclination to reject love. And he has to insist that she accept his attempts to reach out to her and be the leader.

Romance isn't required by God, but if a man wants to give the woman in his life the opportunity to feel like a woman and experience love the way she was made to experience it, he will teach himself about romance and get to work. It doesn't have to be an everyday occurrence, but the occasional romantic gesture goes a long way.

What Is Romantic to a Woman?

For each woman the answer might be different, but here are some places a man can start to find out what kind of romance she craves.

Inexpensive to Free Romance

+ long drives in the country with some of her favorite music on
+ a picnic in a quiet spot, just the two of you
+ a quiet house, music, candlelight, and a foot massage
+ looking her in the eyes lovingly while she talks
+ calling her in the middle of the day just to say, "Hi. I miss you."
+ walking up behind her and hugging her while she's doing something like cooking
+ running her a bath and scrubbing her back (for married men only!)

More Expensive or Time-Consuming Romance

+ taking her to a nice dinner, just the two of you, and not talking about daily drudgeries like work or running the household
+ sending a card and flowers for no particular reason
+ a surprise overnight trip out of town (again, marrieds only, please!)
+ a photo album or movie you make of your years together

14 Loving Who You Want Him to Become instead of Who He Is

Women are very good at spotting potential. Granted, in some cases that might be because there's not a lot more than potential there, but the truth is, they tend to major in it. It doesn't matter if it's putting together a new outfit or designing a new living space, women have the propensity to nest, visualize, accessorize, and make over. When it comes to who a woman picks for a husband, she often sees him as he will be one day. Will he provide? Will he be successful? Will he love her the way she wants to be loved? If he isn't there yet, a woman often just navigates based on the road map she has created for him.

And while many men have great potential, not all of them have an interest in said potential. In other words, *if he isn't who she wants him to be right now, he might never be*. And the Cupidity of it all is that she has fallen in love with an imaginary person instead of the one who is right in front of her. Everyone has potential, but when that's what a woman falls in love with, she's essentially saying, "I'm not in love with you; I'm in love with the future you." While that might make sense and sound inspiring to the female ear, to the object of these so-called affections, it sounds like rejection.

And it is also a bit self-obsessed, isn't it? I'm okay with you, but I'm really in love with my projection of who you could become. You'll do, as long as someday you become more. Ouch. That hurts the masculine heart, which wants to be loved for who he is, not who she wants him to be. When a woman thinks this way, she doesn't have to say anything—he just knows. He knows because there are all kinds of signs that betray her heart. The biggest is that *she has a weird fascination with changing him*. She wants him to wear this instead of that. She wants him to take down that moose head and put up this Monet. She wants him to be more like her—to share his emotions and be more talkative or social. She wants him to have a better job, one that suits her—er, uh, him—better than his current comic-book store managerial position.

She pushes him out of his comfort zone, sure, but he feels a bit like a guy up in an airplane who might consider jumping . . . if the time were right and if he had a parachute. And behind him is a woman who is so confident that he can do it without a chute that she pushes him out of the plane when he isn't looking. Frightening . . . and dangerous. The irony of the whole thing is that **a guy will change if he has a desire to change**. But if he's pressed to change, he will most likely do the opposite and resist. So neither party gets the desired outcome from the situation. It's a lose-lose relationship.

Hayley:

Admiration of who he is today will do so much more for the future him than any brute pressure a woman exerts on his character ever could. Michael has changed so much since we got married. He is more of a man today than he was when we first met, and I adored that man. He has told me, *"You have made me a better man,"* But I've thought, *How can that be? I never tried to change him.* But maybe that's why we've seen so much change—because it was never demanded or even spoken of. If a woman can't accept a man for who he is today, then he's not the one for her. Do yourselves both a favor and don't presume his model comes with "some assembly required." You'll both be happier.

Some Ways Men Feel Disrespected

He does something for her and she says it would have been better if he had done it another way.

He buys something for the home and she looks disappointed.

He makes a decision for the family and she "overrules" it.

She argues with him in front of his friends or the kids.

She complains about him to others.

She is controlling in public.

She criticizes him or his choices.

Loving Who She Was instead of Who She Is

While women are always hoping that things will improve, men are hoping things *won't* change. When a man picks out a woman, he picks out just what he wants and has no delusions about making her into something more. No, he sees a woman, likes her, and chooses her, not imagining her five years down the road—that's too much work. So when she starts to change, he sees the old bait and switch coming on, and he groans. **Men don't see women as diamonds in the rough or worthy renovation projects.** They typically don't find excitement in change but instead wonder, *What happened?*

This can lead to quite a bit of discord when change inevitably starts to happen. There are always areas of change that are going to make a man's life "worse" than it was in the beginning of the relationship. Whether due to natural biological aging or a woman "letting herself go," when the things that were important to him start to disappear, he panics . . . and understandably so. In the areas of looks, sex, and play, men don't do too well when things change, because change usually means "get worse" for him. But a man has

Be the Mirror

When you're single, especially if you live alone, many times it's like going through life without a mirror in your house. You have a general impression of how you look, but unless you feel your face, you're unaware of the pimple that's sprouting there or that you still have bed head. But when you get married (and as a relationship progresses to that end), suddenly there is another person right there getting to know you for who you really are. It's kind of like adding mirrors to the different rooms in your house—first the more public rooms and later the most private ones.

Becoming one flesh with another person is not just physical—that person becomes a reflecting device to show how beautiful or ugly we are on the inside. ***God puts that spousal mirror in our lives to sanctify us and make us better people.*** Just remember one thing: the story of Snow White aside, mirrors don't talk. And even in that case, the mirror only answered the evil queen's questions; it didn't blurt out unsolicited value judgments of what it saw. So be a mirror, not a critic.

to understand that *a good woman is going to change*—physically, spiritually, mentally, and emotionally. Because as believers, we should all be continually improving, and improvement requires change.

The wise man will look at all change in the life of his woman through the lens of God's Word. If her change is more toward holiness and faith, then her change should encourage his own changes in the same direction. But if her change is more toward selfishness and worldliness, then it is his job as a leader to say something. This is important for the woman of God to understand. If her man points out her error—if he sees a change in her that takes her away from obedience and toward worldliness and he points it out—she should be quick to listen and quick to agree with him.

Change is rarely easy, but it is required in the life of one who is striving to become more like Christ. So **men should not be afraid of change**; they should be conscious of it and its impact on the souls of their wives.

Top 10 Things Women Wish Men Would Do

Sympathize; don't fix.

Buy more flowers.

Take her out to dinner.

Take her shopping.

Tell her a song reminds him of her.

Give her cards and notes.

Spend more time with her.

Use hangers instead of the floor.

Put the seat down.

Smell good.

Michael:

I always told Hayley early in our relationship, "I like your hair a lot of different ways—just please tell me you won't get one of those shaved-up-the-back short haircuts." But when Hayley was really ready for a change, I said, "Get a cut that makes you feel good." She got it all whacked off. And it looks great. But I mourned a little bit that my girlfriend, er, wife, didn't look the same as when we fell in love. It was a little thing, but it's an example of how **guys want things to remain the same**. ♥

16

Not Accepting His "Kills"

This might sound like a small, almost insignificant act of Cupidity, but the nuance has such a strong ripple effect that it would pain us to overlook it.

Hayley:

One day, out of the blue, Michael bought me a brand-new laptop. My old one was fine—slowing down, but fine. I was shocked that he would do such a thing. My first feminine impulse was to say, "I love it, but you shouldn't have. You could have gotten a cheaper one. I would have been fine." And so I said it. It wasn't until a few days later, when he wanted to talk to me about something, that I realized something was wrong. In the course of that discussion about our relationship, he pointed out, as authors of relationship books are prone to do, how I handled the receiving of the laptop poorly. *I was completely oblivious.*

I thought it was grace and kindness to almost object to the gift, as if to say, "I don't deserve this." After all, that's humility—isn't it? But it turns out that, in the mind of a man, my humility was a rejection, ever so small, of his kill. He went out like the great hunter he is and found the best beast he could to take care of our family, and I pursed my lips and shook my head as if he had done something wrong. Ouch!

But it makes sense, doesn't it? When you think about it, here he went to the work of doing research and picking out a laptop that would make my work easier, more efficient, and more fun, and the implication was, "You did it wrong. You spent too much; I didn't need this much." It might sound humble to us girlie sorts, but to the man sort it sounds like fingernails on a chalkboard. So learn with me, and the next time a man gives you a gift, *say thank you and give him a hug*. Bite your lip when you want to tell him he spent too much. And you will wipe out one small act of Cupidity that can cause a big heartache in the life of the man you love. 💘

The modern man doesn't need to go out and hunt in order to provide anymore, but that doesn't mean he doesn't kill for his woman. Each day he goes to work and brings home that paycheck, he's bringing home his kill. Each gift he provides, each effort he exerts to make her life better, is the modern man's attempt to slay the best animal and bring it home to feed his family. Without recognizing his efforts as means of provision, many a woman can attack the very calling he was designed for.

Four Ways Women Reject Their Men's Kills

Here are just a few ways a woman can reject her man's kills and in doing so deflate him and even lead him to give up trying to make her happy.

+ When she criticizes any part of the date he planned.
+ When he gives her flowers and she comments that they don't go with the table setting, so she's going to put them in the bedroom.
+ When he gives her anything and she fails to say thank you.
+ When she tells him he works too much, but meanwhile she doesn't control her spending and material wants. Remember, his extra time at work is his way of accepting the responsibility to provide for her. If she really means, "Money isn't important to me," she needs to prove it. When she dismisses the very thing he is compelled to do for her (provide), she leaves him baffled and deflated.
+ When he puts in a new faucet for her and she tells him she wishes he had used brushed nickel instead of chrome.

The more a woman appreciates the hunting prowess of her man, the more he will kill for her.

Eggshells

Walking on Eggshells

Men were made to provide not only financial support and protection for women but also spiritual support and covering, and that cannot be done without occasional admonishment and correction. But many men today have been trained to take the soft way out. They have grown accustomed to only listening and never problem solving. They crave a woman's approval and affection, so they obey the rules *she* has set forth and play by them at every turn. But for a man this is not an act of love but an act of fear and sissy self-preservation. When a man denies biblical truth in order to keep the peace, he is storing up pounds and pounds of trouble for later in the relationship . . . not to mention the possible wrath of God for failing to obey Scripture.

Women today can be heard in all corners of the earth wishing that their men would stand up and be leaders. They bemoan the fact that their men "won't do anything"—that they feel like the man in the relationship and they can't understand where and how they lost their men. ***They want their men to stand up and be men***, but they don't know how to help them or, as many women would say, "make them." It's no question that women, like Eve, have the control thing down. They know what they want, and for the most part they know how to get it, except when it comes to getting their men to step up. The funny (not funny ha-ha but funny stupid) part is that when a man does stand up to a woman, she often doesn't see that as leadership but unkindness, unfairness, or even control, and she rebels. But Rome was not built in a day, and neither is a man's ability to lead. **Through trial and error, men have to learn to lead the women they have been given** (Ephesians 5:23)—or suffer the consequences of failing to provide.

We spend a lot of time counseling people about their relationships, and we are keenly aware of the nasty little fact that women often go to great lengths to punish their husbands. And therein lies their power. All a woman has to do to punish a man is threaten to take away the two most important things in his life, and he's trapped. No surprise, one of those things is sex. The second is less obvious and is rooted in the age-old saying "Happy wife, happy life." It's peace. And it goes back to a man's propensity to collapse on the couch after a day's work. Many a "Whatever you want, dear" has been uttered just to get a moment of peace in the home. So if she's nagging nonstop or, worse, withholding sex, he'll buckle to her control, fearing her wrath (or the absence of her warmth) more than the fires of hell. Sure, he would never say that, but when a guy submits to the control of his wife out of fear, that's what he has proven.

Women cannot be solely blamed for the control they exercise over the men in their lives—manipulation takes two. As we might hear in an episode of *24*, "We don't give in to the demands of terrorists!" Unless, of course, we live with them. Then things get personal, and who wants to give up sex or live in a home with the sound of incessant dripping (Proverbs 19:13)? As long as a man allows a woman to hold something over him, he gives her control. And while peace at any cost might feel like peace, it's really just war with a smile on its face.

When anyone gives in to manipulation and refuses to risk breaking a few eggshells when obedience requires it, they create a world of Cupidity that has the illusion of comfort and safety. But this is a temporary fix at best, because it's impossible to build a strong relationship on the foundation of eggshells. And **life isn't about safety for a man; it's about risk and adventure**.

Human beings don't always know what they need without intervention. Imagine if Adam would have said no to Eve—if he had worried less about doing what she wanted and more about doing what God commanded. Eve might have been angry at first, but the end result would have been far better than the alternative. Maybe Adam was afraid of making her mad, or maybe he didn't want to sleep in his own tree house that night, but whatever his reasoning, his sin has become a problem for all of us.

It can be easy for us fallen creatures to take the path of least resistance. But take that path for long, and you will soon become unhealthy and weak and unable to fulfill the role you've been called to.

18

Refusing to Receive Protection or Correction

Along with provision, it is the responsibility of the man to protect the woman he loves. Even if a woman can take care of herself, she still gives a gift to her man when she allows him—even needs him—to protect her. Face it: in today's world there aren't a lot of things a woman can't do by herself. And many women might even believe they are better at taking care of themselves than any man could be. But an air of "I know how to take care of myself" not only disrespects a man's responsibility to keep his family safe but also says to him, "I don't need you." When a man says, "Honey, I wish you wouldn't do that—it could be dangerous," and she says, "Oh, don't be silly. I'll be fine" and walks off in defiance, she fails to love him. It is the man's responsibility to protect his wife, and when she won't allow him to do so, it is complete Cupidity.

It is the man's responsibility to protect his wife not only physically but spiritually as well. So when a man corrects her for saying or doing something she shouldn't, she would be wise not to give in to her first response to defend herself or to argue. She was given this man to lead and protect her, even from herself, and when he does . . . she bucks right out of the gate? Cupidity. A woman needs to admit that God can speak not only to her but to her husband as well. And she also needs to admit that *she is sometimes so close to herself that she can't see her own mistakes*. Think of it like this: each time she argues with her husband's correction, she argues with God's desire for her to examine her actions and to do all she can to ensure that they are faithful and pure. Is anyone so perfect that they can't take some correction? And even if the correction itself isn't from a faultless source, the willingness to take a closer look is an exercise in spiritual discipline. When a woman subdues her urge to argue, she will find a wealth of instruction and advice that will draw her closer not only to God but also to her husband.

If a woman wants a godly man—one who lives up to his responsibilities, who leads and provides—then she has to consider his advice and correction as more than just another voice in her ear. She has to give him the respect of taking his counsel as good advice and not as an overreaction. When she does, she exercises a delicious side of femininity that is both comforting and exciting to her man.

But what about her own access to God? you might wonder. **Can a wife speak truth to her husband and hold him accountable as well?** To that, many would say yes. And that might be the case, but consider the role of leader. If a woman wants her man to lead, she has to resist her tendency to control him (think Eve). Instead, she must entrust him and his decisions to the One he takes his commands from. When a woman sees an error in her husband, it is always the wisest thing to take it to the Commander himself, rather than to the soldier. Intercessory prayer opens more doors than any other form of communication. If a man is sinning, prayer should be a woman's first response. Consider the fact that sin shuts off his access to the Father (1 Peter 3:12). So when he is out of communion with God, the best thing she can do is to stand up for him and pray that his eyes will be opened and his heart will be softened. After all, whose persuasion is stronger: God's or a woman's? Certainly a woman can feel free to speak truth to her husband, but rebuke, correction, teaching, or criticism will not only usurp his leadership but also lead him to feel unloved, unneeded, and disrespected. The first line of defense should always be prayer.

Hayley:

A Woman's Prayer

I have rarely, if ever, gone to Michael to admonish or correct him. Not that there hasn't been opportunity for it, but I believe in the power of prayer, and I believe that *God holds all the power to influence my man.* If I want significant change, then I go to the Author of change, knowing full well that Michael just might buck from his wife's criticism, but he can't resist the pull of the Lord. Prayer has never failed me! Each time I go to the Lord for help, I am either calmed in my concern, redirected to deal with my own sin, or shown a change in Michael's life that happens between him and God without my having to say a word. Prayer is *true power* for the woman of faith.

Men and women have different ideas of what leads to happiness. When a man is appreciated for all he does, he feels revitalized and strengthened. For a woman, however, appreciation for her hard work is nice, but it doesn't give her the strength to get up and keep moving. She needs communication. And while a man just wants to see the woman he loves happy and content with what she has, a woman just wants him to express the love he has for her in romantic terms. Men and women are different, and if you've never noticed how different before, then maybe you've had a few relationship problems. But the more you not only notice the differences but change the way you behave based on them, the stronger your relationship will become.

If you'd like to see some changes in your love life, now is the time to make those changes. Diagnose the problem and work toward resolution. You have the power to change only you, so start with you, and *start with obedience*. As you look into God's Word and discover how to act in a relationship, what love means, and how leadership affects the way you talk and listen, you will not only improve your relationship but move closer to being the man or woman you were designed to be.

The mind is a terrible thing to waste on Cupidity. Your thoughts on love and the opposite sex have everything to do with how well you love and receive love in return. It is important for you as a believer to know the truth about love and to act on it. You can keep on keeping on in delusion and demands, but it isn't going to get you where you or God want you to be. So free up those brain cells for more important things.

You weren't created to live life in a holding pattern. Get to work growing your mind and soul. That's the only prescription to avoid repeating the Cupidity of your past!

The Pyramid of Needs

Since the dawn of time, both males and females of our species have had needs and wants. And those have never been so clearly seen as in the life of the caveman. Consider Grog's pyramid of needs and how a similar pyramid may represent modern men and women.

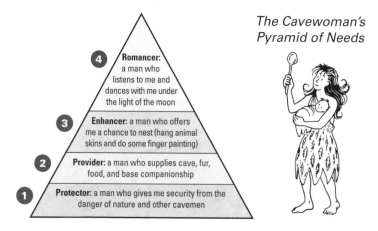

The Cavewoman's Pyramid of Needs

4 **Romancer:** a man who listens to me and dances with me under the light of the moon

3 **Enhancer:** a man who offers me a chance to nest (hang animal skins and do some finger painting)

2 **Provider:** a man who supplies cave, fur, food, and base companionship

1 **Protector:** a man who gives me security from the danger of nature and other cavemen

To build this pyramid, the male of the species has to start moving stones around at the bottom (protector) and build up from there. Once the female gets a level of needs met, she then climbs to the next level and magically forgets about the previous level, focusing solely on the new need. For the man, this can feel like being underappreciated or taken for granted and can cause a lot of grunting and groaning.

Here is the corresponding pyramid for the tribe with the Y chromosomes:

The Caveman's Pyramid of Needs

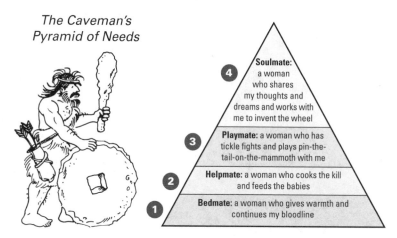

4 **Soulmate:** a woman who shares my thoughts and dreams and works with me to invent the wheel

3 **Playmate:** a woman who has tickle fights and plays pin-the-tail-on-the-mammoth with me

2 **Helpmate:** a woman who cooks the kill and feeds the babies

1 **Bedmate:** a woman who gives warmth and continues my bloodline

When a female learns to start at the bottom of the pyramid and work her way up, she gives her male all he needs to have the most impressive pyramid in the land.

Physical Acts of Cupidity

Believing love is a feeling | Believing romance equals love | Standing on your rights | Misunderstanding forgiveness (or refusing to get over it) | Letting the other person's emotions control you | Thinking that telling him everything is a good idea | Trying to fix things | Taking charge | Failing to provide | Fearing the silence | Refusing to grow up | Failing to notice him | Neglecting romance | Loving who you want him to become instead of who he is | Loving who she was instead of who she is | Not accepting his "kills" | Walking on eggshells | Refusing to receive protection or correction | Using sex to get love | Using romance to get sex | Believing sex will keep them | Withholding sex to get romance | Becoming too comfortable with each other | Shacking up | Enabling abuse | Having friends with benefits | Blending finances before marriage | Giving up food to get love

Loving her for her body only | Dressing to get attention | Looking at porn | Having friends of the opposite sex | Giving too much information | Refusing to move forward emotionally | Letting technology define your relationship | Pleasing the other person at all costs | Disrespecting your significant other in public | Refusing to apologize | Not knowing how to break up | Making a big deal out of everything | Having unrealistic expectations | Wishing your significant other were your gender | Loving someone with a different faith | Expecting another person to bring you hope, joy, or peace | Playing god | Obsessing over yourself | Obsessing over them | Rehearsing the other person's faults in your mind | Sharing sins | Not knowing what true love is

Physical Acts
of Cupidity ♥

If you're the type who craves danger and excitement, it would be best to stick to low-risk things like bungee jumping with dental floss, swimming in shark-infested waters with pork chops in your pocket, or wearing a fur coat to a PETA rally—because those activities are a whole lot less stupid than engaging in physical Cupidity. Emotional and mental Cupidity will get you into hot water. They might leave you forever looking for "the one," or wondering why you married *this* one, but getting physical for all the wrong reasons can have some serious repercussions. As human beings we easily and naturally move from feelings of attraction and excitement into literally "feeling" our way through the relationship. Sex, and all that goes with it, is always out there, knocking at the doors of our hormonally charged bodies and begging us to "get to work." But **we need to listen to more than our bodies**, because the easiest way to commit a really messy act of Cupidity is to use sex for anything other than what God intended it to be.

Sex. God made it. In fact, God made it good! It isn't a naughty thing or a dangerous thing when it's an appropriate thing. But a lot of times sex gets used as a means to an end. And a lot of times that end is the end of the relationship. Whether you are single or married, you have to beware of your own physical acts of Cupidity and how they can mess with your life and your love.

So let's take a look at some physical acts of Cupidity that you may have practiced—or may be engaging in now.

Using Sex to Get Love

In the economy of love, we know there are some things we have to offer in order to get the goods we desire. If what you want is love but you just aren't getting it, sometimes the offering up of sex can seem like a surefire way to get the fire going. Tradition would have it that women are in general the most common culprits of this act of Cupidity, and that's mainly because men will do anything, including offer love (or at least the appearance of it), in the pursuit of sex. Women who use sex to get love have bought the lie that says, ***"If you give me what I want, I'll give you what you want."*** The trouble is that love isn't a currency that can easily be exchanged like the ruble or the peso. *You do this, and I'll love you; you pay for this, and I'll let you have that.* If someone offers love based only on what you give them, then they aren't offering true love but just a cheap, and very bad, imitation. It's like buying a "Rolex" watch on the beach of Tijuana and believing it's the genuine article and will last you a lifetime.

True love is never a payoff for getting what you want. Love, according to God's Word, "means doing what God has commanded us" (2 John 1:6). And we don't have to tell you that God commands us not to use sex to get love (1 Corinthians 6:9-10). It's called sexual immorality, and it ain't good. The truth is that love isn't a feeling generated from something that happens to you, like a sexual encounter. As we've said before, if love were a feeling, then it couldn't be commanded by God. And without question, God commands his people to love (Ephesians 5:1-2). Love is an action, something that *can* be ordered, as in "Love your neighbor as yourself" (Luke 10:27). That means that love, or getting love, isn't based on how another person makes us feel or how that person satisfies our "needs." If we offer love based on conditions, then we are deceiving ourselves. **If we are going to love, we will be able to love someone else even if we never get what we want**.

For the single man or woman, the application is obvious. Having sex just so he won't leave you or so she will say "I love you" is complete Cupidity. *Contrary to a popular idiom, sex doesn't "make love."* If love isn't there before the clothes come off, it's actually less likely to arrive after the clothes are put back on. When sex happens in the absence of love, it's like strapping yourself into a rocket without any idea of where it's going (or if it's even designed to come back). If you think sex will get you love, you're lying to yourself. It's like singing, "Tell me lies, tell me sweet little lies." As if those lies will somehow prop up the walls of your pretend relationship. Not smart.

For the married reader, this concept of using sex to get love has a different twist to it. Once you are married, it's still not about using sex to get what you want, but now it's about offering sex in order to give what you should (1 Corinthians 7:3-4). Sex isn't the thing that will make them love you, but it is what proves to them,

Lies Single Women Believe about Sex

If I have sex with him, he won't leave me.
Sex will make him love me more.
If I don't have sex with him, he'll lose interest.
I'll just do it this once.

Lies Single Men Believe about Sex

You have to test-drive the car before you buy it.
We're engaged, so now sex is okay.
If I'm not having sex, I'm not a real man.
Sex will help me get over my porn addiction.
Everyone else is doing it.

The Two Really Big Lies Married Women Believe about Sex

If my needs aren't being met, why should I meet his?
If I'm not getting it at home, I need to get it somewhere else.

The Two Really Big Lies Married Men Believe about Sex

If my needs aren't being met, why should I meet hers?
If I'm not getting it at home, I need to get it somewhere else.

to God, and to yourself that you love them. Because when we love someone, we want to meet their needs . . . and even fulfill their wants. At the point when you say, "I do," sex becomes a part of the relationship. And as a God-ordained and even commanded activity, it should never be used in order to attain some end, other than becoming one with your spouse and making babies. If you are telling yourself, *I need to have sex in order for him to love me,* you need to make a vocabulary adjustment and start to say, *I need to have sex in order to love him.* Love was never meant to be about me but about us (Philippians 2:3-4). *How can I show my spouse my love?* should always be your first thought. **When giving love becomes more important than getting it, you'll find that getting it becomes a lot easier.**

Love never has to do with anything that contradicts God's Word. So if anything you are doing or thinking of doing goes against God's Word, then you've entered the realm of Cupidity. Watch yourself when it comes to sex and how you use it.

Using Romance to Get Sex

No discussion of physical Cupidity would be complete without a thorough discussion of the counterpart to using sex to get love, and that is using romance to get sex. This is generally a male tactic, as the average female is vulnerable to the fine art of seduction and is often reduced to a willing participant in almost anything if allowed to feel the right amount of romance. That isn't to say that women are more stupid or vulnerable than men, but for most women, *romance has great seductive powers*, and it can easily cloud their vision and their ability to practice self-control. Romance is often the fuel that breaks down a woman's defensive shields and builds up her risk-taking muscles. And that isn't always bad. In the case of a married couple, when romance is used to set the stage and prepare a woman's heart for the next step in the dance of love, it is an amazing thing and part of achieving the union God calls married couples to.

But for the single person, who is commanded to abstain from said union, using romance to get something that is forbidden is an act of diabolical Cupidity. Because this act of Cupidity impacts not only your soul but also the soul of the one you lead into romantically intoxicated bliss. A man is held responsible to God for his actions, so woe to the man who leads another person to stumble and sin against God's law along with him (Mark 9:42). When someone uses romance to get sex, the implications might not be recognizable or identifiable for many years to come. But if you think you can use someone's spiritual weakness to meet your physical need without experiencing ramifications in your future, you are lying to yourself. As a believer, you have to know that one day this manipulative union will haunt you. According to God's Word, **love is meant to be sincere** (Romans 12:9-10, NIV), and that means that romance, if it's a part of love, has to be sincere as well. To a man, that might sound like absurdity—romance isn't love. Ah, but there's the rub: *to a woman, romance is the ultimate expression of love*. When a woman feels romance, she feels love. With each romantic gesture, she falls deeper and deeper. After a night of flowers, dinner, and dancing, she calls her friends and says, "I'm in love!" Just how in love is she? Well, it depends on how good a man is at setting the scene and connecting to her thoughts on romance.

But to all the good guys out there who are saying, "Sex? I would never try to get a woman to have sex with me—that's just wrong," we say, what about using romance to get just a hint of sex? To get her commitment or her "innocent" physical attention? If a man uses romance as a way to get anything from a woman—especially one he doesn't feel he could one day soon love—then he is still abusing the situation and creating a false sense of love in a temporary relationship. Emotional blackmail might be a good word for it. Er, two words. In order to conquer, attain, or be seen with a woman, he might attempt to deliver the romance she craves, but if that romance doesn't come out of a sincere desire to pursue a true love relationship with her, then it's nothing more than a way of extracting payment from a person for something she longs for. Because to the heart of a person—okay, a woman—romance translates as a sincere expression of love. And if that's not what it is, then it's deception. A man who is a believer cannot allow himself to deceive the heart of a woman. It would not only be sinful but also weak and cowardly. Men must protect the hearts and minds of the women in their lives, and when they do, they will develop the skills to love with honor and power.

The Romance/Sex Decoder Ring

If you've made any of the following statements, you just might be hiding your desires in the form of secret code. Which is great if the person you intend to get the message knows the code as well. But if you wrote the code and keep it to yourself, are you really that surprised when the other person doesn't decode you?

Here are some commonly used codes that might be getting lost in translation.

+ You compete to see who can burp the loudest.
+ Farting is an acceptable form of sharing your "feelings."
+ You call each other "the old ball and chain."
+ You say without fear, "You're just like your mother."
+ You never dress up to go out anymore.
+ "Boy, my back/feet hurt." = I could really use a massage!
+ "We haven't been to a movie in a long time." = Can you please take me out?!
+ "I don't have a thing to wear." = Please take me shopping!
+ "I need a cold shower." = I really want a hot shower!
+ "Remember that one time . . . ?" = Let's make a new memory!
+ "Do you have some energy left after your day?" = Let's use it up!

After marriage, however, it is no longer a crime to use romance to get sex. In fact, it would be a welcome gift to almost any wife. In this context sex is usually a given; it's the romance that isn't always there. So for a man to give his wife romance in order to prepare her for what can follow is a generous gift of love.

Another caveat to this line of thinking is the woman who doesn't like romance at all. In relationships where the girl fears romance, you will often find a guy who craves it. The roles get reversed. But in this situation it is rare for the woman to use romance to get sex. If she disdains romance, then she isn't likely to institute it even as a means to an end. But for the romance-craving men who say, "I'm not giving romance to get sex; I'm giving romance because I love romance," we say just be careful that you aren't chasing her off by offering not what she wants but what you want. If she doesn't seem so amped up over the romantic gestures, you'd be wise to take things down a notch and find out what she really wants. In healthy relationships there is a comfortable level of romance for both parties.

Believing Sex Will Keep Them

Ah, the power of sex. A man will do anything for it, it would seem. It's his lifeblood. It makes him feel relief, comfort, acceptance. No wonder he's so eager for any opportunity. Most women understand the value of sex to the men in their lives. And that is where this act of Cupidity gains momentum. If he wants sex, then giving him sex will keep him around, it stands to reason. While this can be true for married lovers, it isn't true for those in dating relationships. If you've done any kind of reading or talking with Christian friends or sitting in a pew, then you are aware that sex outside of marriage is forbidden by God's Word (1 Corinthians 6:9).

That's what we call cheapening God's grace—asking forgiveness before you do something wrong.

Unfortunately, a lot of times God's law gets a pass when his followers rationalize that his grace is enough to forgive their next sexual sin. That's what we call **cheapening God's grace**—asking for forgiveness before you do something wrong.

Don't you realize that those who do wrong will not inherit the Kingdom of God? Don't fool yourselves. Those who indulge in sexual sin, or who worship idols, or commit adultery, or are male prostitutes, or practice homosexuality, or are thieves, or greedy people, or drunkards, or are abusive, or cheat people— none of these will inherit the Kingdom of God.

1 CORINTHIANS 6:9-10

It's using God's grace as an excuse to sin, and it's essentially denying Jesus Christ. As the short letter of Jude warns, "Some ungodly people have wormed their way into your churches, saying that God's marvelous grace allows us to live immoral lives. The condemnation of such people was recorded long ago, for they have denied our only Master and Lord, Jesus Christ" (Jude 1:4). Thinking you have to sleep with someone in order to keep them is physical Cupidity and spiritual stupidity.

Withholding Sex to Get Romance

Once you're married, all of a sudden sex is a good thing. Okay, it's always been good, but now it's *allowed*. You can have it whenever you want. Or at least that's what you thought. But someone else didn't get the memo. For the most part it is a matter of fact that men want a wife so they can get sex whenever they want it and women want a man in order to have full-time romance. **God is good at getting us to live outside of ourselves,** so it's very possible he arranged the sexes to be opposite like this on purpose. What better way to get us to consider and give what others want than to make that the condition for getting what we ultimately want?

Many people believe that marriage is the answer to all their needs. Whatever you dream married life is going to be like before you walk down the aisle is your subconscious list of "needs" that you imagine marriage will fulfill. But God's commands have nothing to do with our felt needs but rather with our spiritual needs. And sometimes those needs stand diametrically opposed. Hence the *sanctifying power of marriage*. One of God's most common ways of sanctifying us—purifying us and making us more like Christ—is in a relationship with a spouse.

But that gift of sanctification is rejected when you refuse to act on God's Word and instead act on what you want. When a spouse withholds sex in order to get romance, they make sex conditional. And while in the world's economy that might sound like a smart negotiating tactic, biblically it's breaking the rules (1 Corinthians 7:3-4). It should be no great secret that blackmail—withholding a good thing from someone until they give you a good thing in return—is unspiritual and self-obsessed. It should be no secret that sexual blackmail is physical Cupidity because it never gives you what it promises to give you. It might seem like your only hope for getting what you want, but in the process it kills the love it purports to represent. And in its place it builds anger, resentment, and distrust, all culminating in a conscious or subconscious desire for retaliation. The bottom line is that as believers our devotion should be to God and his Word above ourselves and our desires. When we set our hearts on what *we* want or on what *we* are lacking, we divert our emotional resources from our desire to love God with all our hearts. And we definitely leave no room for loving our neighbors as ourselves (Luke 10:27).

Most men would be resistant to taking sex from a wife who was unwilling and vice versa, and we would be in agreement. But the truth that every woman and man has to understand is that a husband and wife share the same body when they get married, and just because you aren't getting what you want doesn't mean you can change the biblical rules and refuse to care for your spouse and their sexual needs (see 1 Corinthians 7:3-4 again). For some reason God saw it fit to provide sex as a regular activity between married couples. As with any act of Cupidity, a healthy dose of Scripture, selflessness, and care for the other person breaks down almost every argument to the contrary, and this is no exception.

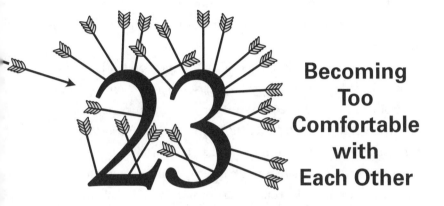

Becoming Too Comfortable with Each Other

When you become close with someone it's normal, even healthy, to become more comfortable with each other. Certainly, once you marry there needs to be a degree of comfort in order to live together. But becoming too comfortable too soon can be a physical act of Cupidity. Have you ever seen a dating couple that acts like an **old married couple**? You might laugh at how they bicker or how they complete each other's sentences. But what about when they touch like a married couple? When the familiarity seems a little too familiar? It gives the impression that something sexual is going on.

We can watch dating couples sitting in the pew at church and by the end of service tell you if they are getting physical or not. Just by observing how comfortable they are together—little physical signals, even in church—we can be pretty sure of their sexual relationship. The more physically comfortable you become with someone you are dating, the more you devalue marriage. There was a day when everything was saved for marriage—when people didn't take naps with each other or stay the night or even go on family vacations together before they were married. They looked forward to a time when they would do all those things as a couple, and it held some kind of mystique. But now couples are playing house and mixing up the order of things before they walk down the aisle.

It might not seem like a big deal, but to the world, it looks like you are lowering the relational boundaries that were once considered proper for God's people. And for the person you are dating, *it takes away a bit of the mystery.* When you're comfortable enough to fart in front of each other, it's time to move up the wedding date, because you've crossed the line into too comfortable. It isn't wrong to let your guard down in front of each other; it can just be a signal of an end to the pursuit and a sense of "arrival." Ah, the aroma of arrival! The chase slows—the couple becomes comfortable, and the relationship becomes stagnant. Many women, especially, can find themselves frustrated by long-term relationships that seem to have no end (marriage) in sight. They say things like, "Why don't you ask me to marry you?" and drop hints or even beg, but what they don't realize is that they've made it too comfortable for him. *Why would he want to ruin things with a ring?*

Consider this: it is the discomfort, the unknown, the mystery that makes the dating relationship so exciting. It offers so much that you can't know for sure the depths of it. You wonder if they feel the same as you; you want to do all you can to please them; you are excited to see them. **Dating is the riskiest time of the relationship,** and out of that risk comes a desire to tie things up—to keep this one from "getting away." When you become too comfortable too soon, you slow down the momentum and delay the ultimate connection.

Hayley:

Too Much Familiarity for Me

I once dated a man I really was into at the beginning. We became close and soon started to become very comfortable with each other. So comfortable that *he didn't think of changing our status.* After we had been together for years I broke up with him, not because he didn't love me or because he didn't want to marry me, but because I had lost the excitement and the mystery that would have led me to say yes. That, and he wasn't Michael! But that lack of initiative, too much time, and too much familiarity without being married drove a wedge between us.

Five Signs You've Gotten Too Comfortable

You compete to see who can burp the loudest.

Farting is an acceptable form of sharing your "feelings."

You call each other "the old ball and chain."

You say without fear, "You're just like your mother."

You never dress up to go out anymore.

Becoming comfortable is an amazing thing. It means you work well together, and it can signal the beginning of a great life together. But becoming too comfortable to match the stage of your relationship can be an act of physical Cupidity. When you decide to allow a bit of mystery to remain, when you remain individuals during the dating process instead of playing house, you give the relationship more of a chance to blossom both while dating and ultimately once you marry. You'll have plenty of time to get comfortable, so don't rush it. Slow things down, and you'll be better prepared to guard not only your heart but also your body in this premarital time of exploration and getting to know each other.

Of course, there is a kind of married Cupidity where becoming too close can be a drawback instead of a marital bonus, and that is in the area of complacency. It's very easy for people to become so comfortable with each other that they neglect the need to impress or even think about one another. When two people are dating, they spend a good deal of effort attempting to please each other. They spend a lot of time preparing for the next date—getting cleaned up, dressed up, healthed up. They work on their bodies and their wardrobes. But something happens when complacency sets in, and that is a disregard for **honoring the other person**. When a spouse chooses comfort over caring for themselves and the appearance that drew their mate to them in the first place, they are putting more value on how they feel than on how their partner feels. In other words, comfort becomes the thing they serve rather than the desires of their mate.

It's healthy to have a good degree of comfort in marriage. We should be able to relax and let things hang out, but there is a difference between being comfortable and being neglectful. If you have let your body go and are a completely different shape than you were when you said, "I do," consider what that says to your mate about your concern for their passion and attraction. Not that you have to maintain the body you had ten years ago, but any effort in the direction of caring for yourself so you can live a long and healthy life together speaks volumes to your mate. Staying healthy and taking care of yourself is a loving gift, one that can pay big dividends in your relationship.

If you feel like maybe your marriage has gotten too comfortable—if you are sensing a lack of a spark and you want more of the attention you crave from your mate—then it's time to check out where you may need to make some changes. It would just be adding more Cupidity on top of Cupidity to put all this on your mate. Blaming them for being so comfortable that they don't notice you or please you anymore is not going to change things for the better. What will make a difference is for you to **become aware of the ways you have let comfort become king**. As believers we aren't called to major on the sins of others but on our own, and we're to remove them as soon as we spot them. Instead of making it about our mates' relational fumbles, we'd do well to ask ourselves, *Am I more concerned about how I feel or about how I can honor them with my appearance?*

Shacking Up

If believing that sex will keep them is Cupidity, then it should come as no surprise that shacking up is utter Cupidity. According to Mike McManus, founder of Marriage Savers and author of *Living Together*, more than eight out of ten couples who live together will either break up before they ever marry or divorce after getting married. McManus writes that, according to a report done by Penn State, **even a month of cohabitation decreases the quality of the couple's relationship**. Many couples shack up in an attempt to save money or to find out how well they get along. This "test-drive" is supposed to give them all the benefits of marriage without the restraint of

> *Let there be no sexual immorality, impurity, or greed among you. Such sins have no place among God's people.... You can be sure that no immoral, impure, or greedy person will inherit the Kingdom of Christ and of God.* EPHESIANS 5:3, 5

commitment. Many people mistakenly believe it to be an insurance policy. A loophole. A way to get around the hard part and just take advantage of the good stuff. But the truth is that this *"practice divorce"* doesn't protect anyone from the ramifications of a commitment gone bad.

The pain from this kind of breakup can be just as wrenching as the pain of an actual divorce.

More than eight out of ten couples who live together will either break up before they ever marry or divorce after getting married.

Practically speaking, shacking up has big ramifications on the family . . . most often on the woman. Children may be conceived in these kinds of situations, and when the relationship starts to deteriorate, it is the woman who is most often left holding the bag (er, baby). Shacking up is a prime opportunity for men to shirk their role as provider, all the while getting a free ride in the bedroom. The main things women need in a relationship—provision and security—are put on hold until the couple decides to marry. While the modern woman might claim it to be a benefit not only for him but also for her, she would be wrong. God has a reason for the laws he has for us, and in this case one of the reasons for forbidding couples to advertise to the world that they are sleeping together without marrying is protection. Protection of the woman and the children. **Real men protect women and children**; therefore, it would stand to reason that real men don't shack up.

A marriage that starts with shacking up is a marriage based on breaking God's law. To say the least, this doesn't give the marriage a very strong foundation to build on. Spiritually speaking, the couple is allowing sin to be part of their daily lives. And they are beginning their marriage hedging their bets against fear and uncertainty. Shacking up betrays a heart set not on God but on the lies of the world that are now deemed "common sense."

Michael:

I wasn't a real man. I shacked up during my bad boy/lame guy years. The funny thing is you're not just playing house, you're almost guaranteed to play divorce court too.

Hayley:

You're not alone. Though it was before I was saved, I shacked up too. It *made sense on paper.* You know, the green kind that's legal tender. But in the economy of the heart and soul, shacking up bankrupts you and leaves a hefty debt in your dating history. This way of life only fed my fear of commitment and my phobia about marriage. In the end, it made my first year of marriage more difficult than it needed to be. Fear became so much my focus that it took some work to get it out of my life.

In a world where living is expensive and relationships are precarious, it's easy to understand why people without faith shack up. But followers of Christ should know better—choosing this road is **reaching for the worst when the best is right in front of you**. It's saying no to the gift of God's help and hand on your life, and deciding to go it alone. "We can be sure that we know him if we obey his commandments. If someone claims, 'I know God,' but doesn't obey God's commandments, that person is a liar and is not living in the truth" (1 John 2:3-4). That pretty much sums it up. It is utter Cupidity to shack up, because it's saying you do not know God. You can't claim to know God and then refuse to obey him in this area simply because it makes sense to you or it seems emotionally safer and cheaper. Willful disobedience isn't covered under grace unless it is confessed and repented from. Choosing to shack up without repentance is Cupidity at its worst.

Enabling Abuse

The mind can play a lethal trick on a person involved in physical violence. While violence has an immediate and painful outcome—one that in general causes a person to recoil and escape to safety—when it is mixed with love or the concept of love, violence can become an accepted behavior. It often starts slowly, like the old twisted science project of putting a frog in water and then turning up the heat slowly so the frog never panics or attempts to get away. But no matter how slowly it sneaks up on you, abuse is always an act of physical Cupidity. When someone accepts abuse, it isn't a way of saying, "I love you, and I understand that you are just angry." It says, "Your anger is more important to me than your soul, and I'm going to let you do what you've got to do in order to placate your emotions." When anger is acted on in a sinful way, it eats away at the spiritual, mental, and emotional lives of everyone involved.

Abuse is never, ever acceptable, and if anyone tells you it is, they are lying to you and leading you into sin. When we refuse to confront sin and instead allow it to control us as we cower in fear,

SIGNS OF ABUSE

According to the Department of Health and Human Services, here are some signs that should alert you to the presence of abuse in your relationship (or someone else's). **If you are with someone who acts this way, it is time to get help.**

+ monitors what you're doing all the time
+ criticizes you for little things
+ constantly accuses you of being unfaithful
+ prevents or discourages you from seeing friends or
+ family, or going to work or school
+ gets angry when drinking alcohol or using drugs
+ controls how you spend your money
+ controls your use of needed medicines
+ humiliates you in front of others
+ destroys your property or things you care about
+ threatens to hurt you, the children, or pets, or does hurt you (by hitting, beating, pushing, shoving, punching, slapping, kicking, or biting)
+ uses or threatens to use a weapon against you
+ forces you to have sex against your will
+ blames you for their violent outbursts

The National Domestic Violence Hotline can be reached twenty-four hours a day, seven days a week, at 800-799-SAFE (7233) and 800-787-3224 (TTY), or online at http://www.ndvh.org.

we are not loving anyone, including God. If you are in an abusive relationship and you haven't considered that you might be allowing sin to be in charge, don't pile on the guilt. *You are not guilty; you have just been sold a lie.* If you are a believer, your body is a temple of the Holy Spirit, so when you protect it you are protecting more than just your body. While it is unbiblical to take on the sins of others and retaliate in kind, it is also unbiblical to allow attacks on the temple of your body. Cupidity says, "He will love me if," but true love is when a man says, "I will love you as"—as Christ loved the church and gave himself up for it (Ephesians 5:25). When a man rejects God's Word in this way, a woman does not have to remain under his abuse. She can leave in full confidence that protecting herself and her family is her God-given duty.

Michael:

Q&A for Men

Q: When is it okay to hit a woman?

A: Never.

There may be a test later in the book. Flunk this one and you may be practicing Cupidity in jail. ♥

If you're married and think it's possible that you're a victim of abuse, talk to your pastor or a Christian counselor who has a high view of both marriage and God's Word. If you're single, you can do the same thing, but our advice, knowing nothing about your situation, is to *get out of the relationship yesterday*. But it's always good to confide in a trusted counselor of God's Word.

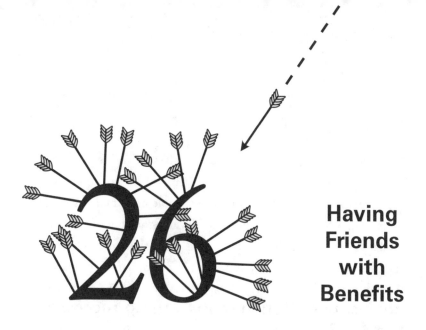

26

Having Friends with Benefits

Cupidity has changed over the centuries, and one sure sign of that is the invention by some devious person (most likely a reality TV producer) of the concept of "friends with benefits." Singles the world over, when faced with few to no prospects for marriage and a tremendous appetite for physical and emotional connection, settle for something that seems safe and easy. They sense a connection between themselves and a friend of the opposite sex, and they see the opportunity to get **all the fun without any of the commitment or effort**. In the friends with benefits model, you have two friends who are happy to have physical touch while avoiding emotional attachment and future plans.

FWB is really an attempt to remove the cause of impatience and the need for long-suffering and to create a placeholder system that makes the delay of marriage more bearable. It isn't always about sex, lest you should think "everything but" is okay. FWB is about all kinds of physical acts like kissing, cuddling, and making out. And for Christians it can seem like an acceptable replacement form of self-control. Feeling the urge? Just call your safe FWB.

And while the world sees no particular problem with such innocent fun (healthy physical release and all), there *are* some spiritual
ramifications. You might not recognize them immediately, but they
are present all the same.

Notice the two main reasons for this kind of relationship:
impatience and lack of self-control. It might be said that those
two scenarios are actually good, though uncomfortable at times,
because they give us opportunities to develop the fruit of the Spirit
(Galatians 5:22-23). The trouble with FWB is that it fails to appreciate the value of sanctification—turning away from the part of
your body that screams, *Give it to me now!* And **it makes the
physical relationship something more like
fast food**: it's not full of nutrition—it's a quick fix. But God
created us for home cooking. He wants us to get all the nutri-
tional value we need in each serving. He wants us to become self-
controlled, not impulsive in our physical urges. And on top of that,
he wants us to value other people more than that. If someone is in
a FWB relationship, they are using the other person for their own
pleasure. And what does that say about the love of God in you?

Friends with benefits leads to all kinds of drama. Undoubt-
edly there will be one person in the relationship who feels a little
more than the other does. And when a love opportunity comes
along—someone your FWB *really* likes—you'll be dropped like a
hot potato. But wait, there's more: as you spend all your free time
getting your groove on with your FWB, you waste precious time
that you could be spending meeting and getting to know a potential real love. Settling for the benefits of the physical without the
context of a committed relationship teaches your heart and your
hormones that being satisfied is the number one objective. It creates the habit of *disposable love*—love that is quickly tossed

aside once better love comes around. It's the foundation of a relational pattern where divorce (or something like it) is acceptable, if only subconsciously, and it doesn't build a practice of committed love. FWB is just another place where you can see the creep of our godless culture integrating into our lives.

Culturally, when there's a group of people satisfied with quick fixes for their sexual appetites, it creates a generation with no commitment to marriage. The focus of relationships then becomes less on meeting the needs of another person, dying to self, and serving them in love, and it becomes more about satisfying urges and limiting responsibility. While being single can be an amazing thing and offer incredible opportunities for service to God, it only works that way if you can control your physical passion. Paul puts it like this: "I say to those who aren't married and to widows—it's better to stay unmarried, just as I am. But if they can't control themselves, they should go ahead and marry. It's better to marry than to burn with lust" (1 Corinthians 7:8-9). **If you feel enough for a person to fool around with them, then marry them.** Doesn't sound good? Then get it right, and stop pretending that your lust is something innocent and spiritually acceptable.

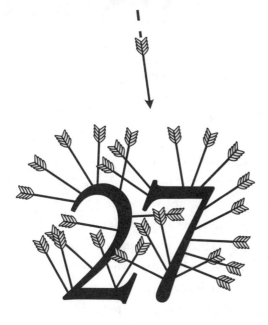

Blending Finances before Marriage

Blending finances before you say, "I do" might not sound like physical Cupidity, but in the same way that flesh is physical, so is money. And when you start talking about blending your money with someone who isn't your spouse, you are talking about physical Cupidity. It's the financial equivalent to shacking up, and it can lead to all kinds of disaster. Buying big-ticket items together because one day you plan to get married anyway is what the old folks call jumping the gun. The problem with jumping the gun is that it sinks important resources into a nonexistent entity. Plus, if you think about it another way, jumping the gun means a firearm is pointed at your rear. **Until you are married, you are not one; you are two.** And blending the finances of two individual people can be dangerous. Not unlike shacking up before marriage, uniting your money in premarital cohabitation is putting the proverbial cart before the horse. It is wanting the benefits of marriage without the commitment.

"But people who aren't married buy things together all the time," you say. "It's called partnership." And to a certain extent you would be right, but they aren't in the same emotionally precarious situation, and usually a business partnership has a written contract similar to a marriage covenant. Coincidence? It might come as a shock, but until you are married, you aren't married. And that means that there is a chance a wedding will never happen. Marriage is the uniting of two people in body, mind, and finances. Dating relationships have a much higher rate of failure. And while a bad dating relationship or even engagement is relatively easy to get out of, when you mingle finances, things become a lot more complicated. Not to mention that expectations tend to rise when two wallets become one before matrimony. And that leaves the door wide open for unrealistic expectations and chainsawing couches in half.

There is, in the acquisition of things as a dating couple, a degree of *"playing house."* When a couple does things typically reserved for married people, it gives the illusion of a deeper intimacy than there really is. Can we go so far as to say that it even might give others the idea that there's "a hint of sexual immorality" (Ephesians 5:3, NIV)? It's the financial equivalent of being overly comfortable with one another, and like too much physical affection between dating couples, it can give the impression that the bond is tighter than it should be. But why should you care if others think you are sexually active when you are not? The answer is simple: people are watching you to see what meets God's standard and what doesn't. When they see acts of intimacy, even financial ones, they make assumptions. And your "freedom" can easily become their stumbling block (1 Corinthians 8:9).

Besides the spiritual side, it's just dumb from a practical standpoint. Watch *Judge Judy* or *The People's Court*, and invariably you see people post-breakup trying to get their stuff back on national TV. What should be a normal breakup (which is painful enough without the added drama) turns into a screaming, petty, divorce-like court case. As a dating couple, you should make it your goal not to get so comfortable with each other that you forget you aren't married yet. When you can give the institution of marriage the respect that it deserves, you'll give *your* marriage the respect that it deserves, and that is priceless.

28

Giving Up Food to Get Love

Okay, so it might be true that the quickest way to a man's heart is through his stomach, but it isn't true that the best way to get his attention is to refuse to eat. Many a guy complains about taking a girl to a restaurant, paying for her big steak and potato, and seeing her pick at it all night without eating it. **There is a certain charm for a man in seeing a woman eat.** It makes her real and relatable. Men love food, and it makes no sense to them why a woman wouldn't feel the same way. But a lot of times women associate food with ugliness. They are afraid to get spaghetti sauce on their faces or have lettuce stuck in their teeth. But what they don't understand is that while that might gross out another woman, we are talking about guys here. The ones who use their T-shirts as napkins. The ones who eat food that falls on the floor. They don't have the same gross-out factor as women. And so when a woman fears food in the presence of a man, it is more destructive than sensible. On the contrary, when a guy sees a girl with a good appetite, it has a positive effect. It's like seeing a woman with an incredible backstroke. It's impressive.

Women often associate food with fat. And fat, according to most women, is ugly, especially when they have to sit on it every day. And so in an attempt to get love, many women starve themselves, hoping that more bones and less fluff will get a man's attention. And while it is true that men are turned on by what they see, it isn't true that all men are turned on by skinny girls. Just as many men are attracted to round, curvy girls. Skinny is a marketing tool for women's wear because it appeals to the feminine eye, not so much the male eye.

Food should never be used as a weapon, either by refusing it in order to punish yourself or by using it to punish the pain you are feeling. Food is meant to sustain life, and any rejection of it is a refusal to care for the temple of God, which is, of course, your body. This topic could be a book in and of itself, but the condensed version is that we have to be very careful not to make food an idol. Any time you give food a high priority in your life, you run the risk of idolizing it. It is idolatry to determine that food is what comforts you or takes away your depression or completes you. Because those roles in your life are to be filled by God alone. And he is a jealous God; he does not stand for rivals (Exodus 20:4-5). When food is worshiped, either by a strict diet or by overindulgence, you have set up for yourself an idol that rivals the golden cow of Moses' era. It should come as no surprise, but practicing idolatry of any kind is like gargling fire—you are destined to get hurt. "You can be sure that no immoral, impure, or greedy person will inherit the Kingdom of Christ and of God" (Ephesians 5:5). ***There is more at stake here than your figure***; there is your soul. And whether you are starving your body or overindulging it, both are acts of physical Cupidity.

If you are using food for anything other than living, then it's time to get some help. The worship or hatred of food is a dangerous thing. And you cannot fully love another while you are obsessed over your own fulfillment or emptiness.

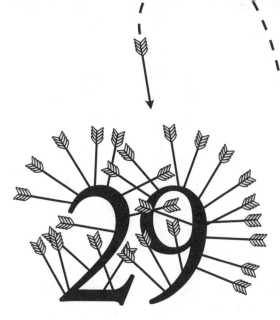

29

Loving Her for Her Body Only

Though there may be nothing more captivating to a man than the female form, it is Cupidity to think that a hot body is all he needs. When men obsess over the physical look of a woman, they run the risk of missing the warning signs that it might not be love at all. A man can become completely blind to everything else in a relationship with a woman whose physical appearance turns him on. And while initially that can be exciting for both involved, ultimately it leaves little room for growth and acceptance. On the surface it might seem like flattery and worship, but it ends up devaluing the woman to the point that she becomes nothing more than an object in her own eyes and in the eyes of her "love."

For the man obsessed with figures (and we aren't talking about accountants here), what does his "soul focus" say about his faith? While a man is wired to notice a nice body, is the physical form really to be the only, or even main, consideration in his search for "the one"? Or does God have something greater in mind? Scripture gives us some insight into *true beauty* that both women who want to possess it and men who want to experience it would benefit from remembering: "Don't be concerned about the outward beauty of fancy hairstyles, expensive jewelry, or beautiful clothes. You should clothe yourselves instead with the beauty that comes from within, the unfading beauty of a gentle and quiet spirit, which is so precious to God" (1 Peter 3:3-4). A focus on the exterior removes the focus from the interior. And for the believer, the interior is the most important thing of all. When a man focuses all his attention on a woman's body, he misses the opportunity to dive deeper into her mind, spirit, and emotions. And over time, if he doesn't do these things, this lack of deeper connection will eventually come back to haunt him. **A man has to truly understand a woman in order to love her.** (Or at least he has to *attempt* to understand her.)

Dressing to Get Attention

This act of physical Cupidity might not seem like such a big deal, but look again. Men are turned on by what they see, and women dress accordingly. And to that most men say, "Bravo!" Face it—there's a reason Hooters is famous, and it isn't just the wings. Men have a hard time saying no to the female form, and women have caught the gist. They use their assets to get the attention of men. "If you've got it, flaunt it," as the saying goes. But when a woman dresses to get attention, it creates a few problems, not only for the men around her, but also for the future relationship that may be born out of her hot bod.

As we said in the previous section, when the body becomes an obsession, it is difficult for a man and a woman to get to know each other deeply. The human body starts decaying shortly after the teenage years—we are all going to age, wrinkle, and break down. So a relationship that is only skin deep will ultimately lead to all kinds of trouble. After all, **there is more to love about a person than what you see**. Besides, the majority of problems in marriage come from the things we don't know or understand about each other. So focusing on how we look rather than on who we are spells trouble in the future.

Unfortunately, women are pretty clear about what gets a man's attention. And so are fashion designers. The acceptable amounts of viewing areas on the top as well as the bottom—and even the middle—have changed a bit over the years. And now it's almost impossible to buy clothes that don't give the world a peek at the girlie parts.

Hayley:

Hayley Revealed

One of us used to show up at church in a short miniskirt, fishnet stockings, and nothing on top but a vest. Okay, it's me, Hayley. *I was a child of the culture.* And I wanted me a man, so those things combined led me to reveal as much as possible. I didn't have a filter when it came to my wardrobe, so my party clothes were also my church clothes. It might be no revelation to you, but when someone pointed out to me the dangers of sexiness, I was completely surprised. I had no idea my body could do things not only to the guys I was trying to get the attention of but also to the guys I would never want the attention of, like the old man sitting behind me or the teenager sitting next to me or the pastor preaching from an elevated position in front of me. I'm not a man—what did I know about skin and lust?

We've both seen our fair share of flesh in the pews. We can remember one time sitting behind a girl who came to church in a beige tank top. From where we sat, we kid you not, it looked like she was naked! Freaky. For a woman, it typically doesn't do much for her to see the flesh of a man, so she tends to underestimate what her exposed flesh does to the men around her. Any guy from thirteen to eighty-eight is having a hard time keeping his tongue in his mouth when a woman walks by with the small of her back peeking out from under her shirt or the top of her breasts gasping for air above her top. Dressing to get attention is failing to appreciate the weaknesses of the opposite sex. It's determining that you can do whatever you want, thinking, *They've just got to learn to deal with it.* That's not only selfish but also sinful. According to Matthew 18:7 (esv), "It is necessary that temptations come, but woe to the one by whom the temptation comes!" If you tempt a man to sin by showing him a little too much flesh, look out, because it would be better to have a great millstone fastened around your neck and be drowned in the depth of the sea than to lead someone to sin (Matthew 18:6).

But let's put the spiritual sin aside and take a look at how it can affect a woman when she uses her body to get a man's attention. Sexy women tend to attract sexual men. While most Christian women might want to save themselves for marriage, many of them are dropping like flies into a sexually permissive pool of honey. There are a lot of reasons for that, but one really practical reason is because when women dress sexually, they create a sexually charged environment around them. And as they do that, men feel like they have permission to be more aggressive and more persistent in their sexual pursuit. When a woman dresses sexy, it's like she's waving a green flag, saying, "All systems go. Prepare to launch the fun bunny." So it should come as no surprise that when a girl dresses sexy, she gets treated sexually. Face it—human beings judge a book by its cover, whether or not that's considered good form. So when a man sees flesh, he considers it **a form of advertising**—an invitation to look, to touch, and to take it home if he thinks it's his style. As we've been known to say, *"If what you are showing ain't on the menu, keep it covered up."* If a woman dresses to get a man's attention, more than likely she'll get the wrong kind of attention—and she just might get more than that.

For the married woman, how she dresses might have slipped her mind. Her husband likes to see her body, so she dresses sexy to please him. But just because she's married doesn't mean other men aren't turned on by her body. Men would do well not to encourage their wives to dress sexy in public. When they do, they completely disregard the spiritual health of the other men she encounters. And while it might make a man feel good to have a hot wife, it shouldn't make him feel good to know what other men are thinking about her.

When a woman wants to be taken seriously—when she wants to stand up for her God, serve him, and love others—she has to make some changes. She has to choose her wardrobe based not on what looks the cutest or the sexiest but on what will bring honor to God and offer the least amount of temptation to the men around her. A woman needs to refuse to walk around revealing the parts of her body that lead men to salivate. Even if they don't see anything until she bends over, that peekaboo view can generate all kinds of sexual thoughts and urges. Dressing wisely isn't a laughing matter or a strange restriction on women, but an act of love that says, "Life isn't about me but about the souls of the people around me."

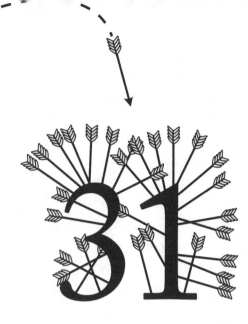

Looking at Porn

What guy (or girl) doesn't know that porn is wrong? If you have any kind of faith at all, no doubt you've heard that looking at porn is a sexual sin. It's the problem of lust. According to Jesus, if a man even looks at a woman with lust in his heart, he has committed adultery with her (Matthew 5:28). It's pretty simple: looking at porn is sin. Any guy who says, "I just can't control myself" is saying, "My 'needs' are more important to me than avoiding adultery." It's a weakness in a man's character to know he has a habitual sin in his life and fail to eradicate it.

If a woman is dating a man who has a porn habit, she can be sure his character isn't what she deserves. When anyone allows a sin to be a part of their lives and claims they are too weak to stop it, it proves their inability to apply God's Word and accept the help of the Holy Spirit. That doesn't speak well for the future of the relationship.

Fortunately, **our God is a God of redemption,** and the good news is that porn isn't a disease; it's a sin. And that means it's a choice. Once we spot sin in our lives, we know we have God's help to overcome it. If looking at porn were something uncontrollable like cancer, then there would be no hope for redemption. But since it is a choice, there is hope. We have seen men steeped in the sin of porn be freed of it by confessing it as the sin it is and choosing a life strategy of repentance and accountability. We can't fit a thorough treatment of porn into this little book, but we want everyone to understand that there are spiritual as well as emotional ramifications of allowing this sin into your life.

Looking at porn is complete and utter Cupidity because of what it does to the mind and the emotions. Porn creates a lie, and it erodes self-control, leading men to replace it with self-obsession. When a want becomes more important than obedience, it becomes an idol. And the worship of this idol endangers not only faith (Ephesians 5:5-6) but also relationships, present and future. Porn doesn't only affect the viewer; *it also affects the one who loves the viewer*. Women are victims of the lie of porn because of what it leads men to think about sex and relationships. When your idea of what is normal and right is set by the standard of porn, you are building your life on a worldly, shallow lie (1 John 2:15-16). And you can be sure that out

> *Do not love this world nor the things it offers you, for when you love the world, you do not have the love of the Father in you. For the world offers only a craving for physical pleasure, a craving for everything we see, and pride in our achievements and possessions. These are not from the Father, but are from this world.*   1 JOHN 2:15-16

of that worldly focus will come all kinds of worldly problems, and the heavenly relationship you crave will never come to pass. For the believer, a godly relationship cannot coexist with the worship of self in the form of pornography.

Physical acts of Cupidity are probably the most obvious of all the types, and there's a good chance you have committed one or two. After reading about them, you may be feeling a load of guilt right about now. But **you can't let guilt be the defining factor**. That's because the main thing is that Jesus gets you and understands the temptations you face. And he went to the cross in order to save you from all your sin and even your acts of Cupidity. The things you have done can't be a cause for self-hate or over-whelming guilt. You can't let them become a reason to give up or to give in again. But you have to know that there is no one righteous, not even one (Romans 3:10). And so your sin is no worse than any other person's on this earth. All sins are forgiven as soon as they are confessed and then walked away from. No matter what kind of mess you've made of your single or married life, there is always redemption—otherwise

Anyone who belongs to Christ has become a new person. The old life is gone; a new life has begun! 2 CORINTHIANS 5:17

Christ died for nothing. Don't make that the case. *The past is the past, and the future can be better* now that you have seen some of the Cupidity you used to call common sense. What you do now will change the pattern of your love life forever.

Nothing—not one act of Cupidity or downright insanity—can

keep you from a new life and a fresh start (2 Corinthians 5:17). No matter what you've done, **it's not too late** to move on. Many have come before you, and many will come after you; you are not alone. You can change the course of your future, starting today. So make a decision to stop the physical Cupidity now, knowing that change takes time, not only in your life, but also in the lives of those you love. Other people might not trust the changes you've made right away, or they might not understand your newfound resolve. But over time and with consistency, the world around you will see and understand the new you. So don't be afraid to embrace change and give in to the power of true love instead of the insanity of Cupidity.

Social Acts
of
Cupidity

Believing love is a feeling | Believing romance equals love | Standing on your rights | Misunderstanding forgiveness (or refusing to get over it) Letting the other person's emotions control you | Thinking that telling him everything is a good idea | Trying to fix things | Taking charge Failing to provide | Fearing the silence Refusing to grow up | Failing to notice him | Neglecting romance | Loving who you want him to become instead of who he is | Loving who she was instead of who she is Not accepting his "kills" | Walking on eggshells | Refusing to receive protection or correction | Using sex to get love | Using romance to get sex | Believing sex will keep them | Withholding sex to get romance | Becoming too comfortable with each other Shacking up | Enabling abuse Having friends with benefits Blending finances before marriage Giving up food to get love

Loving her for her body only | Dressing to get attention | Looking at porn Having friends of the opposite sex Giving too much information Refusing to move forward emotionally Letting technology define your relationship | Pleasing the other person at all costs | Disrespecting your significant other in public | Refusing to apologize | Not knowing how to break up | Making a big deal out of everything Having unrealistic expectations Wishing your significant other were your gender Loving someone with a different faith | Expecting another person to bring you hope, joy, or peace Playing god | Obsessing over yourself | Obsessing over them | Rehearsing the other person's faults in your mind Sharing sins Not knowing what true love is

Social Acts of Cupidity 🩶

While emotional and mental acts of Cupidity are more interior in nature—affecting how you think and feel—social acts of Cupidity, like the physical ones, are most often out there for the world to see. If your life feels like a bad sitcom or a drama that has jumped the shark, then you just might have a case of social Cupidity to contend with. It is those moments when who you are on the inside comes blurting out into the open, and everyone gets a peek at what makes you tick. Social Cupidity is definitely the **most embarrassing kind of Cupidity**, because it's so often a form of foot-in-mouth disease.

Social Cupidity always involves the expression of your character, either verbally or nonverbally. So it can show off some pretty nasty stuff—like refusing to apologize, giving too much information, or making a big deal out of everything. It's all those things that can make your life a *social disaster* and knock the love right out of the air and onto its tiny heart-shaped back. So take a look at these acts of social Cupidity and see if there are any that have you acting like a relationship dummy.

Having Friends of the Opposite Sex

It's not out of the ordinary for people to have close friends of the opposite sex. Just looking at three decades of TV programming—*Three's Company, Friends, Will and Grace*—it seems to be the norm for boys and girls to be friends. So what's the great Cupidity in having friends of the opposite sex? Let's start with single Cupidity. If you are single and reading this book, then we are going to assume that you don't want to be single forever. And if that is the case, let's just say that being good friends with someone of the opposite sex is what we call **"delay of game."** That's because that need you have for companionship and many other things that come with marriage are met in your friendship—with a few big exceptions, of course. So not unlike the couple who is having sex before marriage, taking what isn't theirs and pretending that it is, coed friendships can take what isn't really yours—intimacy with this person—and pretend it is.

Hayley:

Time for a story. When I was single, there was a time when my closest friends were two guys. I spent every day with at least one of them. We talked on the phone and shared our passions, dreams, and defeats. We went dancing, dining, and shopping. If you saw me out with either of them at a restaurant, you would have assumed we were dating. Now, I also had another friend—a not-so-close friend, but a friend all the same—who was a member of the female gender. And she started to date one of my guy friends. They hit it off and started seeing each other every day. Even though we were all friends, I was a third wheel most of the time. And so *I lost one of my most intimate friends*. When they broke up, I got him back, but shortly after that I found Michael and the process started all over again—but this time in reverse. By the time I got married, I had lost both of my best male friends.

Doing dating stuff, such as going out together, talking on the phone, or hanging out at home with someone you aren't romantically interested in, creates all kinds of opportunities for Cupidity. *Friendship with someone of the opposite sex is simply pseudo-dating.* Let's compare it to the movie business. You know what a stand-in is—that person who kind of looks like the star but isn't and who stands in the scene while the cameramen are doing the boring stuff so the star can go rest in their trailer? Yep, the stand-in: **all the work of the star but none of the stardom, pay, or perks**. It's a lonely position, except when all the eyes are on you, and then maybe for an instant you can pretend that you really are the star. At least until you get your paycheck, that is. That's the condition a lot of singles find themselves in. If you are friends with someone but you really are wishing and hoping there could be more, then consider yourself a stand-in. You might have visions of becoming the star of their heart, but the chances are slim. As soon as they audition a candidate who foots the bill, they'll be gone—too busy to give you the attention you've gotten used to.

So consider this dynamic and then weigh the fact that in opposite-sex friendships, one of the two people often wants to **stop being a stand-in** and start making the big relational bucks. Maybe it's not you who wants more; maybe you just don't want to be lonely or to show up without a "date." Maybe you like the benefits of the friendship, whatever they are, and you are using the relationship to take the sting out of your singleness. And in doing so, you are using the person. Even if you both confess that there are no feelings involved, the chances are slim that is true for both of you. And even if it is true, when one of you mates up, the other one will be left holding the lonely bag.

"But we can still be friends," you whine. Well, let's just say for laughs that your significant other would have no feelings of jealousy or insecurity about your being closer to your friend than you are to them. Let's just say that they won't envy your intimacy and feel somehow less close to you because someone else of their gender knows more about you than they do. Let's just say that. But once you get married, the whole game changes. It is marital Cupidity to think that it's okay to bring your opposite-sex friend into the relationship with you. It's like keeping your boyfriend or girlfriend while you're married, and it's creepy. Especially if this friend was once more than a friend—then it also becomes disrespectful. The spiritual danger in the whole thing is that when you are that close to someone, you often go to them when times get hard. So what happens when things get rough with your mate and you run to your BFF? Well, the potential for trouble is endless. You are intimate, you know each other well, and they don't yell at you or argue with you. They don't resent you or tell you what to do. Suddenly that person is looking good, and in a moment of weakness you both crumble. And *bam*, adultery. Even if nothing physical happens, it's still cheating on your mate if you go to another person for the emotional needs they were meant to fill.

So let's just spell it out: *if you are married and you haven't left your close friends of the opposite sex behind, it's time for a breakup.* Your spouse might never have made a peep, but we can promise you that they are jealous on some level—or at least they should be. They want what you and your friend have, and they wonder if it will ever go further. That's not love; that's selfishly holding on to what you want or what you believe you need, all the while forgetting that you are to consider others—especially your spouse—more highly than yourself. As believers, we have a different set of rules than the rest of the world. We are called to "do nothing out of selfish ambition or vain conceit, but in humility consider others better than yourselves" (Philippians 2:3, NIV).

Giving Too Much Information

In a relationship with the opposite sex, it's important to understand your audience. If you want to connect—if you want them to like you and to like being with you—then you have to understand what makes them happy and learn what you might be doing that takes away their happiness. In relationships, most *women bond by talking*. No big secret. Whether in love or friendship, if women don't talk they feel like there is no chemistry, whereas two men can get together and sit on the couch, watch a game, and go home having said no more than a handful of words, and feel like they had some good male bonding.

In chapter 6 we talked about the assumption that telling him everything is a good idea and how men don't do well hearing all of a woman's complaints and pains. Giving too much information is similar in nature, and it can happen to both men and women who share too much of their lives with a new "friend" too soon. For a woman, this often stems from the false assumption that the more quickly she helps him know and understand her, the more quickly he will fall in love with her. In other words, she assumes

Male Bonding	*Female Bonding*
watching TV	talking
playing ball	shopping while talking
destroying something	creating while talking
building something	going to a movie and talking
driving something	eating while talking

he's a girl. Sure, he wants to get to know her, but he's a dude, so he'd be happier with smaller amounts at one sitting. It's kind of like water. Drinking water is essential—you'd die without it. But give a man too much water and he'll drown in the very thing he needs to survive.

Hayley:

Michael and Hayley's First Date

While it's often women who love to communicate, the same problem can come up when a man gets too communicative and dumps his entire life on her in one sitting. *Too much information is too much for a reason.* Both sexes like a bit of mystery, and when you say it all as fast as you can, the mystery is gone.

When we went on our first face-to-face date, Michael did all the talking. He dumped his entire, messy life on the table for me to examine. His intentions were good; he didn't want any false advertising. He wanted me to know what I would

be getting into if I dated him. He was trying to protect me,
really. But it felt like too much information to me. So by the
end of the date I was ready to go. On the phone with my
girlfriend later, talking about the date, I said, "I don't think he
likes me much. All he did was talk about himself."
A woman wants to talk, and when a man dominates the
whole convo, she doesn't feel a connection. Men, too,
would do well to consider mystery as they get to
know a woman. 🖤

So what exactly is too much information for a woman to give to
a man? Well, while in the beginning stages of the relationship, she
might do well to consider any of the following subjects to be TMI:
her health, her cat, her mother, her PMS, her wardrobe, her ex, her
favorite soap opera, anything that pegs her as a complainer, and
her desire to be married, make babies, and decorate a home. The
trouble with this kind of sharing is that it takes away the chance
for him to chase her. It's like the difference between finding a car-
ousel horse and running after a wild horse. Which one sounds like
a more exhilarating challenge for the male's need for adventure?
Too much information and he's going to feel like he's going around
and around on a pink pony with a painted-on saddle. Yawn. But if
a woman wants to encourage some mystery in her life, if she wants
to intrigue him and draw him in so that he says, "I want more,"
then she's going to have to practice what we call **the fine art
of shutting up**. It's a technical term, but this is a technical
problem.

So what about for him? What is TMI for a man to give on a
first or second date? Here are some things that don't need to be
discussed early in the relationship, no matter where they are on

his "needs" list: when he wants to get married, how many children he wants, how his last girlfriend treated him, how to change the manifold on a GMC Jimmy, the difference between digital and analog, how much he loves your mother (or hates her), his high school football glory days, how to field-dress a moose, or any other in-depth explanation about something he is good at but she has no interest in. The trouble with this kind of info is that he will either scare her off with his speed of emotional attachment or make her feel unneeded in a conversation that's all about him and his hobbies. *A woman wants to be romanced, not educated,* on a date. So he'd do well to enjoy being with her, talk about light and fun things, and avoid getting all "professor" on her.

As we talked about in #6, the problem of TMI can exist in marital Cupidity as well. Sure, the woman has him now, and he should know everything about her. But you should also drink eight glasses of water a day, and chances are you don't do that all in one sitting, right? So she needs to slow it down on the information bath. He needs to know her, yes, but she shouldn't drown the poor guy. A good rule of thumb is that when he walks in the door at night, she shouldn't look at that moment as a chance to finally have adult conversation or a captive audience. She shouldn't look at it as a chance to put him to work—he just got off work. Instead, she should give him some peace and let him have a heads-up: "There is something I want to tell you after you've had some downtime," or something like that. She should be less eager to force him to listen and more confident that most of her complaints and dumping would be better made in her prayer closet. That way God can shoulder her load and teach her how to slow down and be satisfied even when things aren't going her way. A woman's other ally in the area of conversation is her girlfriends. A good girlfriend can be a marriage saver, because a friend can handle the major load of her word count, giving her man a bit of a break when it comes to the art of listening.

Women can have a tendency to believe that men are just like them and capable of going nonstop. But that's primarily a female trait. Women are compelled to be busy; men do all they can not to be busy. **He isn't a girl, and she should be glad for that.** And part of being glad that he's 100 percent man is appreciating that he does life differently from the way she does. How great it is that God saw fit to design us as opposites. If a woman was looking for the male version of herself when she married, then she married out of Cupidity. But have no fear—Cupidity can be reversed. It does, however, take a conscious effort and her desire to appreciate all that is male in her man, all the while understanding that saying no to herself and her longing to dump on him is an act of spiritual discipline (Philippians 2:4).

Move Forward

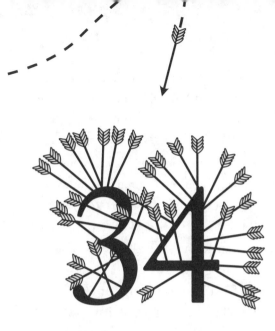

Refusing to Move Forward Emotionally

As in everything, young grasshopper, balance is key. Too much information and not enough are just two sides of the same coin. And neither will do anything productive for your relationship. Refusing to give of yourself emotionally tends to be a male condition, but there are women who suffer from this form of emotional constipation too. There's something to be said against emotional dumping, but little by little you need to allow yourself to be drawn out. That's where the balance issue comes in. Giving information about how you think and feel is essential to a healthy relationship, and it has to be done with love and a concern for the other person's needs. When a man refuses to move forward emotionally, **he can hold a woman hostage to her own need for connection**. This emotional blackmail leads to all kinds of crazy thoughts and even actions on the part of the woman. Many women just leave when they realize that things are going nowhere, but others hang on to the hope that one day things will all change and he will suddenly become emotionally available.

For the person who has trouble expressing his feelings, try this progression: start talking to a houseplant. If you don't have one and think you might just kill one if you did, buy a fake houseplant. Now take some time alone, just you and Fern, and practice opening up. See how Fern is a good listener? At first you're going to feel crazy (and you are), but just have a one-way convo with Fern. Then an amazing thing is going to happen. Soon enough you'll begin wishing Fern would respond so you could have a *back-and-forth dialogue*.

Once you master sharing your feelings with flora, it's time to move to the animal kingdom. Dog, cat, whatever, as long as it's some sort of living mammal. It will feel eerily similar to Fridays with Fern, but now you are dealing with a creature that has some sense of free will and most likely a very short attention span.

Your final step in stretching your expression muscle is practicing (without their knowledge) on a friend or coworker. It isn't always the case, but many times problems in communicating feelings aren't confined just to romantic relationships. Be adventurous and stretch yourself in both emotion and vulnerability with this "safer" person. And then, congratulations! You're ready to feel out loud in public!

Five Signs You May Be Emotionally Constipated and Need a Relaxative

You've been dating exclusively for over a year and you
   haven't yet said, "I love you."

When she expresses her love, you reply, "Ditto."

It's been over three years, your age doesn't end in "teen,"
   and you can't commit.

You refuse to meet the other person's parents or family.

You can't say the "*M* word" in conversation.

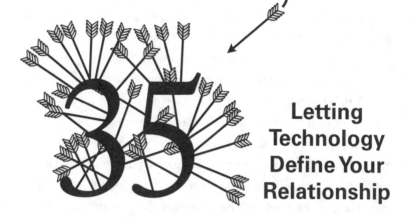

Letting Technology Define Your Relationship

There was a time when communication was slow. Love letters took days, even weeks, to get to their destination. In order to talk, you had to be in the same room or the same pasture. But now communication has exploded and gone from slow and sparse to instant and continual. Technology can be a huge benefit to relationships, but it can also be a hindrance. Texting, Facebooking, Twittering, IMing; what's a person to do with so much access to the object of their affection? Special attention has to be paid to make sure technology doesn't become so intrusive that it alters the state, quality, and proper pace of the relationship. So here's some help for you tech lovers out there who want to enjoy easy access without becoming too emotionally easy.

For the most part, **men love to chase**. That means that men should enjoy setting the relational pace and making the emotional advances (i.e., making the first contact and chasing the woman to get her attention). While there isn't necessarily a biblical command telling women to let men do the chasing, there is a good deal of common sense to be found in understanding that women can easily overdo communication and access at the hands of technology. In order to have fun playing chase, there needs to be one person chasing and one person being chased. If the chasee doesn't pull away at least a little from the chaser, there's no chase to be had. It's like a game of tag with no one running. So when it comes to technology, here are some good ways to make sure that TMI and TMA (too much access) don't damage your relationship.

Texting can be easy and addictive, but too much of it, and it can become smothering and mystery defeating. If a man is texting throughout the day, a woman would be smart not to respond every time. When she responds quickly to every one of his technological advances, she sends the message that she is waiting by for his next contact—doing nothing else and having no other life. Though that may be exciting to the guy for a time, *eventually it will become like mannequin tag*. So the woman needs to slow down on the response time to give the man a chance to wonder what she's doing and when she's going to respond.

Now for our male readers. You need to know that texting can be something women look forward to, but too much and you destroy the excitement as well. There is a good deal to be said about the thrill of the unknown, and over-texting can destroy that. So men need to strike a balance between overdoing communication and avoiding it altogether.

Also, brothers, don't go friending every cute girl on Facebook, followed by "What's up?" Don't forget, your prospective Betty sees everyone else you've poked, SuperPoked, and digitally prodded on your wall. And if 90 percent of your FB friends are women, umm, diversify.

Likewise, ladies and gents, don't be a Facebook wall stalker. Don't be the guy who has to comment on every update she posts. Don't be the girl who always asks, "Who's Jenny?" or "Who's Carla?" or "Who's Granny?" **Insecurity is ugly.** It says, "I'm desperate, and you're the only person I think I can get and keep." Yuck.

The real danger for everyone when it comes to technological communication is its addictive nature. It is Cupidity for anyone to obsess about the next status update or Twitter feed. To be healthy in your relationship, you've got to keep a good perspective and appreciate the value of patience and the slow reveal.

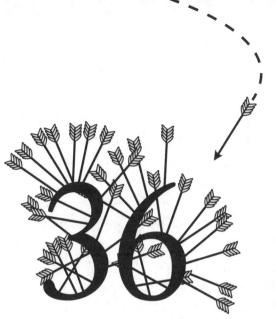

Pleasing the Other Person at All Costs

When it comes to love, the job description is simple: think more about them than you do about yourself. It's what gives you the ability to love selflessly. And it's one of the hardest things you'll ever do—especially when it isn't as simple as pleasing them at all costs. It's about pleasing them in ways that are pleasing to God. People pleasers are actually less concerned with loving the people they please and more concerned with self-protection. If you base your success as a mate/boyfriend/girlfriend, or even as a human being, on what the other person thinks about you at any given moment, you're in for some heartache, because emotions, like the stock market, rise and fall. If your ultimate goal is pleasing people instead of loving them, then you have a social act of Cupidity on your hands. The trouble with making it your goal to please people is that it places the real focus not on the person but on yourself and your fear. You fear that they will get mad, reject you, leave you, or criticize you. It is said that *perfect love drives out fear* (1 John 4:18). If fear is the impetus behind your desires, then you aren't showing real love.

Okay, so maybe you say your pleasing tendencies aren't done

out of fear; you just don't like disappointing people. Then the next question is, what happens when you disappoint someone? If your answer has anything to do with you and how they will look at you or treat you, then you're a people pleaser. Busted! So let's consider the concept of being a people pleaser and how it ultimately disappoints. When you take your car in to the mechanic, do you want him to be a pleaser or a truth teller? Would you like your financial adviser to tell you your portfolio choices are great just to appease you, when you are actually investing in a square tire company? So why should love be any different?

Love isn't being a yes-man. It isn't doing whatever someone wants just to keep the peace or to fulfill their desires even if those desires are inappropriate, impossible, dangerous, or unbiblical. What the people pleaser has to do is check their motives when their instinct is to agree with or do whatever another person says. Are you acting out of fear or faith? Saying no isn't always a bad thing. We say no to our daughter's desire to have candy after every meal, and though she might think that's mean, we know the truth—that it is done in love. Is it easy to hear her whine and complain about how it's "not fair!"? No, but that doesn't give us a pass on standing up in love and doing what is best, not just what is desired.

Lest you think we are contradicting our earlier suggestion that you seek and act on what makes the other person happy, this kind of pleasing at all costs perverts the giving nature of love into a warped kind of getting—getting some peace and quiet, getting to go to bed without a fight, getting sex, etc. One person in the relationship is more concerned with what they get out of the equation than with how best to love the other person. It's taking the idea of giving what makes them happy to the extreme and disregarding the concept that sometimes no is the best thing a person can hear.

When a woman is a people pleaser, she tends to take on more than her fair share of the workload in order to care for everyone. Her need to nurture and serve explodes, and she finds herself running ragged trying to meet everyone's needs and wants. *Busyness is often a sign of the people pleaser.* She gets so busy that she has no time for spiritual devotion and rest. Her inability to say no prevents her from choosing the model of God to rest at the end of the day or in the morning. It also leaves everyone in her life feeling frazzled, rushed, and exhausted, since the pace of the house and the family living in it is primarily set by the woman. And if she is a people pleaser, she will tend to overwork not only herself but everyone else, too.

When a man is a people pleaser, he tends to act out of his male desire to provide and make others happy. When a woman nonchalantly expresses her dissatisfaction, the people pleaser is quick to jump into action, and he can also be just as quick to resent the fact that he's being called to work again. Like the busy people pleaser who resents her own busyness, the afraid-of-not-making-you-happy people pleaser resents the very person he is frantically trying to please. In this situation **he puts so much value on making a woman happy that he buries his command to lead her**. He might feel she is disrespectful in her requests or treatment, or that she's refusing to submit to his headship, but the truth is that he is living one of the lies of Cupidity.

Consider this: if you are doing something that your mate/ significant other wants because you want to please them, but all the while you are steaming about it, then you are suffering from pleasing at all costs. The motive of your heart is what is really at stake here. They may never know how your heart steams over your giving, but you can be sure that God does, and he sees not love and selflessness but sinful emotions like bitterness and resentment. If those are creeping into your heart, you have to ask yourself how to either accomplish what you want in true love and peace or consider what you are resenting and if there is a legitimate underlying problem—something that isn't good for your family or your relationship. It is a difficult equation to resolve, but through prayer and time in God's Word, you will become more true to the heart of love and less focused on pleasing at all costs.

Deep down the people pleaser knows when their attempt to please is unfaithful and when it is genuine. The best litmus test for pleasing at all costs is the presence of sin. If you are lying, disobeying, or acting in any sort of sin, it's time to reassess what love means to you and how better to live in it. If the person you love is sinning and you are going along with it to avoid confrontation, then you've crossed the line into helping another to stumble.

You Might Be a People Pleaser If . . .

You think saying no is mean.

You think everyone has to like you.

You resent saying yes to things, but you agree to them anyway.

You fear being disliked more than anything else.

You tolerate mean or disrespectful behavior in others in order to keep people from leaving you.

Sometimes you care more about what people think than about what God thinks.

37

Disrespecting Your Significant Other in Public

Never, ever, ever disrespect your significant other in public. This social act of Cupidity tears down the heart of your loved one and destroys any love they felt you had for them. For women this is *a particularly dangerous pastime*, especially since God commands women to respect their husbands (Ephesians 5:33). When a woman complains about, insults, or orders around her husband in public, she is turning her back on God's command and driving a big wedge between herself and happiness. Henpecked, spineless men—men who don't stand up and take a lead, who ignore their wives, who don't act chivalrously—are usually the ones who are disrespected in public. The thing for every woman to remember is that another person's sin is never a free ride to sin herself. His sin doesn't excuse hers. Whether the woman is standing beside her husband or on her own, talking negatively about him is destructive to him and to the relationship.

The same admonishment goes for men. If a man disrespects his wife in public, he is breaking her spirit. Any love he offers her in private will disappear under the pressure of his disrespect. Mocking her, complaining about her, or pointing out her weaknesses is of no use other than a lame attempt to build himself up. His job as a man is to love her as Christ loves the church. When he disrespects her like this, he rejects God's Word and runs the risk of losing access to the very God he claims to serve (1 Peter 3:7).

For couples who are dating, consider this: if you are being disrespected by the object of your affection, know that it will likely get worse, not better. You have the chance to **get away now, while the getting's good**. Disrespect, especially in front of others, is a bright red flag telling you the race is over.

Disrespect is heartless and selfish and fails to take into consideration not only God's Word but also the mind and heart of the

Four Ways a Woman Disrespects Her Man

criticizing his provision
fixing something he has already fixed
flirting with other men
fawning/fantasizing over celebrity men

Four Ways a Man Disrespects His Woman

criticizing the way she keeps house
flirting with other women
commenting on the beauty of other women
not calling her when he's going to be late

one you love. If you have disrespected your loved one in public, you have only two things to do: apologize and repent, refusing to do it ever again. Of course, don't rub salt in the wound by telling them all the times you disrespected them that they don't know about. That's just adding more disrespect onto disrespect. Getting it off of your chest doesn't do any good to anyone but yourself.

Refusing to Apologize

Some people are under the misguided notion that an apology is a strike against them—as if saying, "I am sorry; you were right" or "I'm sorry I hurt you" makes them look bad. It can feel like a loss when you admit mistakes or bad behavior, but the truth is that an apology does more to soften the heart of those you love and to draw them back into trust and faith in you than sticking to your guns ever could.

Michael:

I'm Sorry, but I'm Not Sorry

In the early part of our marriage, Hayley didn't know how to say, "I'm sorry." In fact, she believed it was not an appropriate response. She would ask forgiveness if she sinned or did something to hurt me, but if it was something that didn't require forgiveness, **she wouldn't apologize**. Now something you need to know about Hayley is that she is a bit of a klutz.

She is under the illusion that it's endearing—her trips and spills and stomps—and there was a time early on when she was oblivious to what it did to me. I don't know how many times she would accidentally kick me, scratch me, or step on my bare feet with her boots and never say, "I'm sorry." I used to think she was uncaring and unloving, but after a few years I talked to her about the importance of apologizing, and a light went on. She had never been taught the simple courtesy of saying those little words. And when she finally got the importance of them to me, our fights diminished dramatically. ♥

Hayley:

I Really Am Sorry

It was an odd expectation to me that when Michael was getting mad at me for something, he often simply wanted me to say, "I'm sorry." He didn't want an explanation of why I did something or why I didn't mean this or that. He didn't want "excuses," which to me were explanations. All he wanted was a simple "I'm sorry" so the misstep of my big boots could be acknowledged and we could move on. At first I bucked at the prospect. *"Why should I apologize when I didn't do anything wrong? It was a total accident."* But slowly I started believing in the power of apology, and I found myself saying, "I'm sorry" with less and less difficulty. I used to think it was like losing a point off my scoreboard. But it turns out it is a huge win, because his potential irritation softens and the argument stops right where it is. My old way of explaining myself just drew out the fighting more and more. 🙢

When a person does something to hurt, inconvenience, or disrespect another, **an apology is always the best policy**. If you really want to drive home your regret over your mess-up, then ask them to forgive you. This gets them actively

Apologizing with *Flair*

Need some help apologizing? Here are four ways to do so with flair. (Just remember, they have to involve saying, "I'm sorry!")

For Women

+ Write, "I'm sorry" in lipstick on a mirror.
+ Tuck a note into his pocket or briefcase.
+ Bake a huge cookie with "I'm sorry" or "ILY" written in chocolate chips.
+ Respond playfully to everything he says with "You're right!" for thirty minutes.

For Men

+ Draw a picture of flowers. (Buy flowers for happy occasions.)
+ Learn how to say, "I'm sorry" in her favorite foreign language (and say it).
+ Create a time line of the sorriest people in history. Insert yourself at the end.
+ Rent an animal costume and dress up as the "Armadillo of Sorrow."

involved in the apology and allows them to offer you their grace in the situation, similar to the grace we experience from God on a daily basis. Refusing to apologize is Cupidity because it protects self at all costs and determines that *being right is more important than being happy*.

Not Knowing How to Break Up

Have you ever dated someone way past the relationship expiration date? Or broken up with someone only to end up back together after their tearful pleadings? Breaking up hurts, there is no question, but what hurts more is not doing it when you should or not doing it correctly. Many people believe that lying is far less distasteful than hurting someone's feelings or being alone again. And because of that they pretend to be into the relationship when they desperately want out.

Hayley:

The Slow Breakup

I used to be the queen of breakup malfunctions during my dating years. I feared hurting someone's feelings more than anything else. I was also afraid I wouldn't find another man if I broke up with the guy I was in a relationship with. I once dated a guy for five years because I was afraid to walk away.

What if there isn't anyone better? I worried. I loved him deeply, but I wasn't in love with him. He was my best friend, not my future lover. But still I clung to the hope that things would work out, even when it became clear that I needed to let him go. *Fear kept me leading him on.* I wish I'd had the strength to hurt him earlier so that the pain would have been more bearable instead of waiting five years to do it. I really regret hurting such a good friend. ❧

Of course, this is a singles' act of Cupidity. Once you are married, there is never again a need to know how to break up. Because breaking up post-marriage isn't an option (Mark 10:11-12). We date in order to ultimately find true love—the person we will be with for the rest of our lives. So *refusing to break up out of fear is just delaying finding true love.* And not breaking up when you know it's time is not only cruel but also selfish. It might feel like the exact opposite, but refusing to let someone go now, when you know eventually it will have to be done, is determining that how you will feel when you break it off is more important than letting them get on with their lives. The key to breaking up is to care enough about the person to do what needs to be done without fear (or in spite of your fear).

Maybe you have no fear of breaking up; you just have no skill at it. If you tend to break up badly or, worse yet, you try to break up but don't make it stick, then it's time to learn how to break up the right way. The thing to remember is that **breaking up is your choice**, and because of that it should have nothing to do with the other person's pleading. In order to have a good breakup, you have to be confident and direct. You can't say, "I think I want to break up with you," because that just gives them an open door in

Pharisees Ask a Question out of Cupidity

Some Pharisees came and tried to trap [Jesus]
with this question: "Should a man be allowed
to divorce his wife for just any reason?"
"Haven't you read the Scriptures?" Jesus replied.
"They record that from the beginning 'God made them
male and female.' And he said, 'This explains why a
man leaves his father and mother and is **joined to
his wife**, and the two are united into one.' Since
they are no longer two but one, *let no one split
apart what God has joined together.*"
"Then why did Moses say in the law that
a man could give his wife a written notice of
divorce and send her away?" they asked.
Jesus replied, "Moses permitted divorce only as a
concession to your hard hearts, but it was not what
God had originally intended. And I tell you this, whoever
divorces his wife and marries someone else commits
adultery—unless his wife has been unfaithful."
Matthew 19:3-9

which to stick their foot. You can't give them any spot where they can debate you once you've made your decision.

One of the biggest mistakes people make when ending a relationship is the gradual breakup. It might seem easier to "take some time off" or to slowly stop calling them and seeing them or to try to be "just friends." But each of these attempts to ease the sting of breaking up only makes more relational trauma for both of you and should be avoided. (If you can find a copy of our book *The Art of Rejection*, check it out.)

If you happen to be on the receiving end of the breakup, it is Cupidity to whine, beg, or refuse the breakup. The best thing to do is to accept the other person's reasons and then **say good-bye**.

You have to allow them to have their own opinions and desires, and you need to realize that you cannot truly change anyone or convince them to love you. Any attempt to do so will only make things worse.

Breaking up is almost an inevitability in the life of a single person, so you need to be prepared for it and not fear it. Remember, each breakup leads you one step closer to finding "the one."

A Reason **Is a Reason** *Is a Reason*

People tell us one of the major reasons they're spending a lot of time thinking about a breakup before it actually happens is because they are trying to figure out how to defend their reasons to the rejected party. So let's see if we can help speed up the process by looking at two major categories for calling it quits: little things and deal breakers.

Little Things
   body odor
   the sound of their laugh
   eating habits
   nervous tics
   their wardrobe choices
   Diet Coke over Diet Pepsi

Deal Breakers
   wanting kids versus not wanting kids
   where they ultimately want to live
   different lifestyle and financial goals
   difference of faith
   lack of chemistry
   no evidence of love (includes things like abuse,
      lies, and destructive behaviors)

You might be thinking, *Oh, great, I've got to come up with a deal breaker.* Wrong. There is no unspoken rule that you can't break up over one little thing. As hard as it might be for the rejected person to fathom, something seemingly small like body odor, the sound of their laugh, or any other little thing is enough to pull the plug if you say so.

You don't really have to have a reason other than that you just don't feel like dating them anymore. It's your life, your choice.[1]

---

[1] Adapted from Hayley and Michael DiMarco, *The Art of Rejection* (Grand Rapids, MI: Fleming H. Revell, 2006).

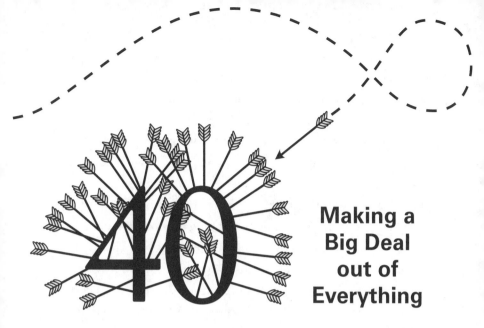

Making a Big Deal out of Everything

The propensity to blow things out of proportion is generally a characteristic of the more feminine or sensitive person in the relationship. That isn't a slam on femininity but a commentary on the primarily female tendency to take things personally. *Women are made for relationship*; they thrive on it. Soap operas and reality shows are so big in the female demographic because they give viewers the feeling of being part of a story that is bigger than themselves. The female inclination to overanalyze emotions, words, and actions isn't a stereotype for nothing.

After a three-hour phone call between a dating couple, the girl hangs up and calls her friend. They then rehash the previous conversation for another three hours, analyzing everything that was said and dreaming or worrying about what he meant when he said _____. The guy gets off the phone, sits down on the couch with his buddy, and plays Xbox without saying a word about the marathon call other than, **"That girl can talk!"** Because women are so keenly aware of social nuances—because they watch and listen so intently and care so much about communication—they tend to be the ones who make a mountain out of a molehill.

Making a big deal out of everything is kind of like always being in overdrive—your engines are always revving and you are forever hot. Or it's like frying your potatoes on high and then being surprised when you burn them. If you are a believer, life should mostly be made of little deals, not big deals. That's because believers practice faith, not fear. We believe that if God looks after the sparrow, he'll surely look after us (Matthew 10:29-31). And we believe that if we who are sinful give good gifts to our children, how much more will our God give good gifts to us (Matthew 7:9-11)? As believers, we know that God works all things together for the good of those who love him (Romans 8:28). So how can anything—even the worst disaster in the world—be a big deal in comparison to God's bigger plans? Understand that we aren't trying to minimize your pain here; we just want to set it against the backdrop of the bigger picture in order to put suffering in perspective.

When someone makes a big deal out of everything, it is very unattractive to those who are watching. Essentially it is saying, *"I don't trust you, so I'm going to freak out now."* Beyond that, it implies, "This is all your fault." Remember that for a man, his number one job is to provide for the woman he loves. And if her life is falling apart, even if he had nothing to do with it, he still feels responsible. It's part of his nature. The crux of this particular act, for a man or a woman, is the failure to think about the heart of another; instead, it puts all the focus on one's own heart. It's an easy thing to do—seeing things from your perspective and never from another's—but it's still Cupidity. Love doesn't look inward at feelings and wants but outward at the condition of others. Love empathizes and steps outside of itself, all the while trusting God and recognizing that freaking out and making every-thing a big deal isn't the way of faith.

If it's your nature to make everything a big deal and you are freaking out right now, relax—that's to be expected. It's a habit, and it takes time to change a habit. It takes time to realize your error, confess it, and then turn around in the opposite direction and refuse to do it again. But God promises to help you; you aren't alone (Philippians 4:13). If anyone can help you **stop the cycle of worry** and take the focus off of yourself, it's Jesus. So relax and trust, and you'll be all right.

Hayley:

I Married a Slob!

How many women would agree? The messy bathroom, the clothes left on the floor, the dirty dishes just dropped in the sink—why doesn't he pull his weight around here? It can be easy to blow this particular "weakness" out of proportion. *I asked him to take out the garbage a week ago, and it's still there! Does he not smell it when he walks in?* And your anger seethes. The truth is, no, he doesn't smell it. And he probably doesn't even see it. Maybe it is a divine gift that allows men to overlook mess and discomfort in favor of trekking through the forest and sleeping on the dirt, all to make the kill and bring it home for the family's survival. Maybe if men had the same cleanliness sensibilities as women, they couldn't live in the trenches, collect our garbage, clean our sewers, survive the stench of war, or do any other of a million dirty jobs without complaint. *Thank God for men!* So the next time you complain about your husband's inability to carry half the load of housework, instead stop and thank God that he made him so *rough and tumble*, manly, and able to do the dirty work. And the next time he kills that big spider for you or fights off the wolves, give him a big hug and thank him from the bottom of your tidy heart.   ॐ

Michael:

Minimizing Everything

So Hayley and our editor, Stephanie, are making a big deal during the editing of this manuscript about the primarily male tendency to minimize everything. They think it's really important to include another chapter addressing that to balance out this section. **I don't see what the big deal is.** Sure, when a guy minimizes everything, he makes himself look superior while the woman looks like a bat-crazed emotional loon, but what's the big deal? I mean, sure, it drives a wedge between the male and female lovebirds, but it'll pass, right?

Maybe it's like he sees everything as a pothole instead of the Grand Canyon, which is good, yeah? He can dodge one or two potholes driving the Ferrari that is the relationship, but if he fails to patch enough potholes in his communication, his once sweet ride will fall to pieces. And no one wants to lose his Ferrari. Wait, what were we talking about? Whatever, it's probably not that big of a deal.   ♥

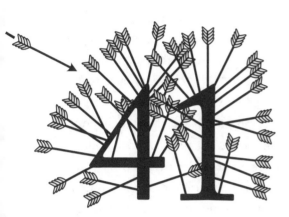

41

Having Unrealistic Expectations

If you find yourself saying the following expressions a lot, then this section is for you.

"Why didn't you do what I asked?"

"Why do you keep forgetting to do that?"

"How could you be so dense?"

"I get no help around here."

"What were you thinking?"

When the people you love disappoint you, you can start sounding like a perpetual nag. Some women complain daily that he won't put his clothes in the hamper or lower the toilet seat. They wonder why he steps over the broken cookie on the floor instead of picking it up. And men ask, "How many times do I have to tell you to let me know the *day* the 'check engine' light comes on instead of a week later?" or "Why can't you weigh the same as when we first started dating?"

The higher your expectations of a person, the further that person can fall and the easier it is for you to be disappointed. To clarify our terms here, this isn't a conversation about godly and good expectations, like a woman's expectation that her husband should get off the couch and get a job, no matter how much below his pay scale or pride level it is, or a man's expectation that once he's married it means he can have sex regularly. No, we're talking about those *silly little expectations* we all have that are more about making our lives easier than about true responsibility. If your spouse doesn't cut the mustard in areas that are important to you but not scriptural in nature, it's time to start evaluating whether they're realistic or demanding. This perspective is important, not to give them a free pass because they are too stupid or lazy to get it, but to help you calm down, gain your composure, and stop the bitterness and resentment that unrealistic expectations can bring on.

It is a lie to tell yourself that another person should do just what you say, when you say, and how you say. That is called being a **puppet master**, and it requires nothing less than physical control or brainwashing. But if we aren't mistaken, you didn't marry a robot or a little bald man wearing a saffron toga and bowing every time you walk into the room. Freedom is an amazing thing. If your loved one didn't have freedom to choose and act on their own volition, you'd never be sure if they truly loved you, because they would be powerless to do anything but. It goes back to the old argument for why God would allow his people free will when he knew we would just mess it up. It's because *he wants genuine love to be a choice, not a preprogrammed involuntary response*.

And so in pursuit of love, it should come as no surprise when people don't obey our every command, read our minds, and act on what we are thinking. We should expect opposition, differences of

opinion, and even different wants and needs. Once we stop believing what others should and shouldn't do and think instead about
what *we* should and shouldn't do, our relationship traumas will be
on the mend.

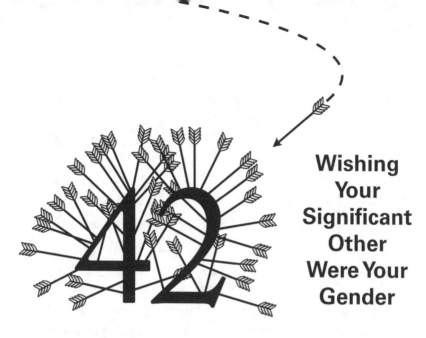

Wishing Your Significant Other Were Your Gender

Okay, this might sound like a homosexual thing, but it isn't. Just stick with us. When you are dating or married to someone, you realize what you are getting, right? You are getting someone who, at the core of their chemical makeup, is significantly different from you. Every time you cringe or, worse yet, complain when they do something completely foreign from what you would do, you are buying into *the false assumption that you are with the male or female version of yourself.* If you believe they are going to want all the same things you want and react the same way you react, you are bound to be disappointed.

Hayley:

Would You Rather Marry a Girl?

Women often come to me upset over some guy thing their husband did. They say things like, "He gets home from work and he doesn't want to talk about his day" or "Why

doesn't he want to spend the day shopping with me?"
I always want to say (and occasionally do), "Well, would you
have rather married a girl? Because that would take care of
that character trait."

The opposite sex is so, uh, well, *opposite* that it can feel like the clash of the Titans whenever they do things specific to their gender. But complaining about the gender traits of your spouse is like, in the words of John Miller, author of *QBQ!: The Question behind the Question*, looking at a soaring eagle and saying, "I wish he could swim the seas like a dolphin." Silliness. But silly we are when we look at someone God made with specific gender traits and wish those traits were more like ours. Why won't he go shopping with me? Why isn't he neat? Why doesn't she want to watch sports? Why won't she climb on the motorcycle with me? **Whenever you bemoan your significant other's gender, it is Cupidity.** Instead of noting the differences and calling them problems, why not appreciate the differences and imagine your mate having all the bad habits of the opposite sex? Imagine your woman scratching herself inappropriately in public, or imagine your man chattering a million miles a minute, searching for a belt to match his wallet, and complaining that he has nothing to wear. You might just get a laugh out of it and begin to appreciate again their differences instead of being exasperated by them.

Committing social Cupidity can be embarrassing once you realize what you're doing. But that's just the beginning, isn't it? Because then comes the backlash. If your social life is less than you dreamed it would be, it might be time to take stock of some of the relationship habits you've fallen into. The good thing about being a human is that **you have the power to change the patterns in your life**. So don't get down, but get to work, doing something to correct your social breakdowns. As you start to work on them, don't be surprised if your significant other isn't participating or even buying the new you. Remember, it takes time to prove to others that the change is for real. It's only through repetition that they're going to finally get it. What counts right now is that you want to make a change and start to love the right way, ditching your former ways of Cupidity and getting smart at love.

Spiritual Acts of Cupidity

Loving her for her body only | Dressing to get attention | Looking at porn | Having friends of the opposite sex | Giving too much information | Refusing to move forward emotionally | Letting technology define your relationship | Pleasing the other person at all costs | Disrespecting your significant other in public | Refusing to apologize | Not knowing how to break up | Making a big deal out of everything | Having unrealistic expectations | Wishing your significant other were your gender | Loving someone with a different faith | Expecting another person to bring you hope, joy, or peace | Playing god | Obsessing over yourself | Obsessing over them | Rehearsing the other person's faults in your mind | Sharing sins | Not knowing what true love is

Believing love is a feeling | Believing romance equals love | Standing on your rights | Misunderstanding forgiveness (or refusing to get over it) | Letting the other person's emotions control you | Thinking that telling him everything is a good idea | Trying to fix things | Taking charge | Failing to provide | Fearing the silence | Refusing to grow up | Failing to notice him | Neglecting romance | Loving who you want him to become instead of who he is | Loving who she was instead of who she is | Not accepting his "kills" | Walking on eggshells | Refusing to receive protection or correction | Using sex to get love | Using romance to get sex | Believing sex will keep them | Withholding sex to get romance | Becoming too comfortable with each other | Shacking up | Enabling abuse | Having friends with benefits | Blending finances before marriage | Giving up food to get love

Spiritual Acts
of Cupidity ♥

Spiritual acts of Cupidity might be a lot less obvious than those social acts, which are out there for the whole world to see, but that doesn't make them any less deadly. Because what you believe about God and the spiritual life has an ultimate impact on how you behave in love. In fact, we could have called this entire book *Spiritual Acts of Cupidity*, because as believers, ***everything we do is based on how we view God***. But for this chapter we will be talking specifically about those acts of Cupidity that involve your spiritual life—things like accepting sin as the cost of love, encouraging each other to accept less than God's best, and refusing to live up to our spiritual responsibilities.

For true believers, there is no such thing as keeping your faith and your love life separate (Colossians 3:23). When Sunday is a distant memory and your emotions are on their last legs, it can be hard to think and act spiritually, but that's the point. **Faith proves itself not in the easy times but in the hard times.** You don't test your strength with three-pound dumbbells but by lifting heavier weights today than you lifted yesterday. You don't go up a grade level by passing tests on last year's subjects. You improve by digging in and learning new stuff—stuff that will bring you closer to your goal. It can be easy to just relax in what you know about love without reaching out to grow and try new things. But *love never stops learning*. Since you're never going to be perfect this side of heaven, you've got to keep striving toward your goal. "I have not achieved it, but I focus on this one thing: Forgetting the past and looking forward to what lies ahead, I press on to reach the end of the race and receive the heavenly prize for which God, through Christ Jesus, is calling us" (Philippians 3:13-14).

The following descriptions of spiritual Cupidity might get you worked up more than any of the others you've read so far, but that's normal with issues of the soul. Don't refuse what shocks your system at first, but take a chance and see if there's anything here that might just be what you've been looking for in love and in life.

Loving Someone with a Different Faith

A lot of single people talk to us about their confusing love lives. One of the biggest confusions seems to be who to date and who not to date, especially when it comes to the realm of faith. It's hard enough to know if this one is the right one without having to diagnose their spiritual condition too. But it's worth giving consideration to, because **the biggest causes of fighting in relationships are sex, finances, and differing views on faith**. And for the believer the latter should be the biggest warning signal around. If the person you are interested in doesn't have the same faith as you, then the red flags are flying, the stop signs are dancing, and the roadblocks are up. Dating—and marrying—outside of your faith is setting yourself up for mental, emotional, and spiritual disaster. If you are a believer, the core identifier to your life is the belief that God is God and you aren't. Your faith in who God is according to the Bible doesn't allow for you to marry someone who doesn't have the same core beliefs as you. People who have fought the system and married outside of their faith anyway will tell you that it makes everything in life harder when they don't worship the same God their spouse does.

When you love and worship a Being your partner denies the very existence of, it is difficult to be true to yourself and your God. *You become torn between your two loves.* One wants you to do and say one thing, and the other wants another response. We have counseled countless people who have grieved the situation they created after having children with their unbelieving spouse. They were left struggling with what faith to give their kids and wondering whose influence would win out. When God is truly the Lord of your life, it is sheer Cupidity to marry someone who doesn't hold the same value system. In fact, it is a decision that goes against the very Word of God, which says, "Do not be yoked together with unbelievers" (2 Corinthians 6:14, NIV).

But loving on different faith levels isn't just about marrying a nonbeliever. The person you love might claim to believe in Christ and call themselves a Christian. But if you confess that Christ is Lord of your life and have made it so, then you have to be discerning about how you accept other people's proclamations of faith. See, the Cupidistic part is that even the demons believe in Christ (James 2:19). They've seen him and they know he's real, but that doesn't make them Christians.

If you have any question, if you are wondering in any way, if the faith of the person you're dating is as deep as yours, then you have to acknowledge potential trouble. **Those instincts of faith can't be ignored.** Romantic love can cause you to overlook a lot of things, and sometimes that's for the best, but in the case of faith it's for the worst. It is Cupidity to believe that your faith will change theirs, and especially to believe that you'll eventually lead them to Christ. In some circles that's called missionary dating, or trying to get someone saved so you can get what you want—their true love. But it's a dangerous tactic. Oftentimes the nonbeliever will make a pretend conversion, where they say what you want so that they can get what they want—you. And then after the "I dos" are said, you're stuck with the harsh reality that their confession was coerced, not genuine. If God is truly the most important thing in your life, you can't become one with someone who disagrees with you. Because when you become one, that will mean that you have cut your devotion in half.

But *what if you're already married to a nonbeliever?* Is there any hope? You might feel isolated, lonely, depressed, and fearful about their eternity, but there are some things that are important to realize in that situation. Just because you messed up, it doesn't give you permission to divorce your spouse in an attempt to clear the slate. That would just be messing up again (1 Corinthians 7:12-13). And though you might want to drag them to church and tell them to sit down and shut up, you can't do that either.

In many instances the nonbelieving partner is a man. And the important thing to know about a man is that if he is told to do something, he will generally do the opposite. He doesn't appreciate being ordered around, so when he feels the hand of control, his first impulse is to rebel. So even if his wife is just asking him every Sunday, "Would you like to go to church today?" he takes that as her attempting to control him. In these situations, the woman can't do what comes naturally and take charge—she has to let go and do what God wants her to do so that he can take charge. And this is what God expects: "You wives must accept the authority of your husbands. Then, even if some refuse to obey the Good News, your godly lives will speak to them without any words. They will be won over by observing your pure and reverent lives" (1 Peter 3:1-2). It's a hard pill for a woman to swallow to think of submitting to a nonspiritual leader, but it must be done. This can be a chance for a woman to exercise faith in the face of seemingly insurmountable challenges. The most important thing for her to know is that everyone is watching how she will respond, including her husband, family and friends, and kids if she and her husband have any. A woman can't resent the fact that he is the same guy today as he was when she picked him.

This is a harsh discussion to have, and not many people are brave enough to do it. We are, though . . . because you can't slap us or tell us we are horrible friends. Ha-ha! But according to those who come to us for help, that's what makes us good counselors: we aren't too close to the situation and we aren't just trying to make you like us. We really want you to understand and live God's Word, even when it hurts.

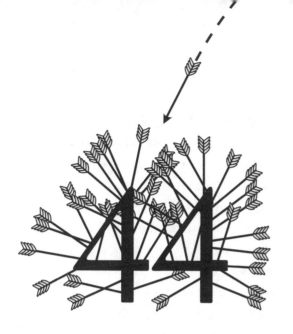

Expecting Another Person to Bring You Hope, Joy, or Peace

A lot of acts of Cupidity are perpetrated in the name of expecting another person to bring us hope, joy, or peace. It's probably the most common mistake of the single person looking for love. When we look for love, *we all believe in some part of our hearts that when we find it we will have arrived.* After all, we think we've found the person who will bring us the joy of love, the hope of a perfect life together, and finally the peace that will put our chasing and loneliness out to pasture. But it is spiritually dangerous to put so much expectation onto another human being. To both people in a relationship we say, "Your job is to make the other happy," but to both of them we also say, "Should that never come to pass, you can't claim foul play." You can't demand love or anything that goes along with it, and for that matter you can't even expect it. Jesus says, "In this world you will have trouble" (John 16:33, NIV). He expects us to find it pure joy when we face trials of many kinds (James 1:2). And he wants us to trust that our present trials and suffering are nothing compared to the glory that awaits us (Romans 8:18). So to expect a mate to eliminate all of life's difficulties and disadvantages is spiritual Cupidity.

When you put your hope solely in the hands of another person, you are sure to be disappointed. That isn't because there is no hope but because your hope is to be somewhere else. And when your hope is heavenly focused instead of humanly focused, you have all the hope you need (Romans 15:4). Surely we should all be hopeful in love; otherwise we'd be a bunch of emotional misfits. But it's too big of a burden on another human being to put all your hope on them and expect them to provide what only God can provide. The same is true for joy and peace. We find those things in our surroundings and in the people we love only insomuch as we put our faith in God and trust that obedience to his Word is what brings us true feelings of fulfillment.

When Jill puts all her hope in Jack, she soon becomes very angry when he disappoints her. She resents the fact that he doesn't provide the emotional high she dreamed of. His moments of relational weakness leave her angry and bitter. His inability to completely "get her" dashes her joy and becomes her rationale for declaring war. And Jill becomes sullen and bitter. She doesn't smile much anymore. She refuses to do anything and spends much of her time sulking in the bedroom. She blames him for his humanity and makes it her destruction. After all, he should have been the source of all her bliss, she thinks to herself. And Jill isn't alone. (In fact, there are a few Jacks who have fallen into the same trap.) *A lot of people mistake romance and marriage for paradise*, and then after they say, "I do," they realize they had it all wrong.

It is complete Cupidity to believe that another person, no matter how "perfect" they are, will be your salvation from a life of testing, suffering, and purification. In fact, the opposite is true. The beautiful thing about marriage is not that it gives you everything you've ever dreamed of but that it gives God a prime opportunity to sanctify you. And if you recall, he doesn't do that through happiness but through testing and discipline. No one is more able to speak to the sins and blemishes in your life than a spouse. And if they are willing to do that in love, then you have found something even better than marital bliss.

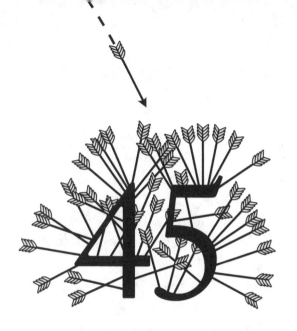

Playing God

So be honest: have you ever thought how much fun it would be to be God? To have all the right answers at all the right times, to know exactly what everyone should do and when they should do it? How much fun ... even if only to be god of your home, god of your relationships. After all, you don't need the whole universe or even the whole block—you're too busy as it is. But what if everyone in your little circle of influence understood that you know best and didn't argue with you about anything? Ah, heaven. Playing god isn't an unusual pastime. Like the five-year-old who plays house with her sister and imagines that the plastic food on the plate is steaming hot and edible, it's easy to forget that you aren't infallible when it comes to your decisions, wants, and needs.

It's like this: you have a tendency to roll your eyes when someone you love does something stupid. As if you wouldn't ever have done something like drop the ketchup bottle on the floor, causing it to spray the fridge and the cabinets with red goo. Or when they forget to pick up what you needed from the store and now, as you loudly remind them, "No one will be able to eat!" **It is playing**

god to pass judgment on others as if you don't do the very same things yourself (Romans 2:1).

Men have to keep up their guard against this so their call to lead does not become confused with the call to rule over creation (Genesis 1:28). To rule over someone is to demand allegiance, but to lead the way Christ led is to be fearless in the pursuit of holiness and generous in the offering of grace.

One way a lot of women are prone to play god is by believing that *everyone's well-being is their responsibility*. (This doesn't include kids, of course, because they are a parent's responsibility, but a spouse, other adults, coworkers, and friends are not.) When you fret over the choices and lives of other adults as if you know better and you wonder how they could do such a thing, you are betraying your hankering to play god. If only you could be the chess master and move the pieces around the board without so much rebellion and fighting. Things would be so much easier. When a woman believes that others outside of her care can't do life without her intervention, she not only abuses her relationship with them but also attempts to remove from them the very suffering and trials God intended to help them to grow.

When you see trouble or strife, especially as the result of sin, you have to consider God's hand in the situation. He disciplines those he loves (Hebrews 12:6), and any attempt on our part to remove another person's struggle would be like opening a cocoon in order to rescue the butterfly trapped inside. Do that and you'll end up with an anemic butterfly that can't even flutter its wings, let alone fly.

There is only one God, and it ain't you.
Remember that Satan's fall came because he wanted to be God. When you attempt to control others or believe you are the only

one who can do something that needs to be done, you come dangerously close to sounding like a guy with red horns and a pitchfork. Ouch!

SIX SIGNS
YOU MIGHT BE PLAYING GOD

Every time someone you love does something wrong, you have to confront or correct it.

You think the louder you talk
the more people will listen.

You often demand an explanation for others' behavior.

You are just bossy by nature, and you expect
everyone else to deal with it.

You believe everything would fall apart
without you.

You think you are the only one who can
do whatever needs to be done.

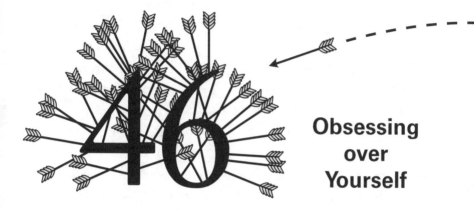

Obsessing over Yourself

If you've ever loved someone who was self-obsessed, we feel your pain. It has to be one of the most frustrating and painful relationships you can have, especially if you really care about the person. Self-obsession can come in many forms—being arrogant, not listening, making it all about *me*, whining, complaining, arguing, controlling . . . you get the picture. Self-obsession is simply being so focused on your own needs, wants, and dreams that you ignore or even step all over those same things in others, including in the people you purport to love. Toby Keith said it best in response to a self-obsessed person: "I wanna talk about me. I like talking about you, you, you, you, usually, but occasionally, I wanna talk about meeeeee." And in this section, that's exactly what we'll be talking about: you. All you. It's not so much about loving someone who is self-obsessed; it's more of an inward peek at yourself. After all, self-obsession is hard to spot, just by definition. It's all about **giving in to self**, not looking soberly at self. Self-obsession is a spiritual act of Cupidity because it is a refusal to accept the biblical command to humble yourself.

All those things that place you at the center of the conversation—your needs, wants, and heartaches—are spiritual Cupidity when they get lopsided and become mostly about you. When you think about all the amazing people you know or have heard of, the thing about them that most often captivates other people is their ability to live outside themselves and to serve the world around them. Think about who is more appealing, even as a friend: the person who is with you 100 percent when they are with you or the one who is forever looking around at other things going on while you are talking? The person who is always bringing the subject back to themselves and their life or the one who listens to your story and actually comments on it? And so, being a good friend and getting back to you, let's take a look at how you can go from being the distracted lover to becoming the selfless one.

Don't be selfish; don't try to impress others. Be humble, thinking of others as better than yourselves. PHILIPPIANS 2:3

In biblical literature there is not a clear distinction between humility and meekness or patience.
TYNDALE BIBLE DICTIONARY

Self-obsession was never the character of Christ, who said, "Take my yoke upon you. Let me teach you, because I am humble and gentle at heart, and you will find rest for your souls" (Matthew 11:29). Here Jesus describes himself as gentle and humble, and we are commanded to be the same. "Don't be selfish; don't try to impress others. Be humble, thinking of others as better than yourselves. Don't look out only for your own interests, but take an interest in others, too" (Philippians 2:3-4). So *humility is the answer* to this brand of spiritual Cupidity.

How directly this stands in contradiction to what the world considers smart or even healthy! Of course, humility isn't a call to a life of being the victim—it isn't honoring to God to allow others to abuse his temple that is your body. It is a call to emotional and mental meekness, which involves refusing to allow the sin of others to become a source of your own sin. It involves **refusing to become the victim** by allowing the actions of others to control you.

Meekness: enduring injury with patience and without resentment
EASTON'S BIBLE DICTIONARY

According to God's Word, self-*anything* (well, except self-control) isn't a biblical mandate and most certainly isn't obedience.

It's like we tell our three-year-old daughter: "You can whine all you want, but you aren't getting what you want." God says the same thing: You can fight, claw, argue, and put your hands on your hips all you want, but that won't get you what you want. Never. He will always sit you back down.

Until you submit yourself in humility, you'll continue to get what you are getting. If you want God on your side, if you want him to hear your prayers, then you have to die to your urge to be heard and instead choose obedience. His Word confirms it: "The eyes of the

Humility: a socially acknowledged claim to neutrality in the competition of life BRUCE J. MALINA

Lord watch over those who do right, and his ears are open to their prayers. But the Lord turns his face against those who do evil" (1 Peter 3:12).

If you want a change in your life, in your relationship, then now is the time and this is the place. You can change it all . . . by changing yourself, how you think about yourself, and how you interact with the person you love. Will you have a self-obsession or a God-obsession?

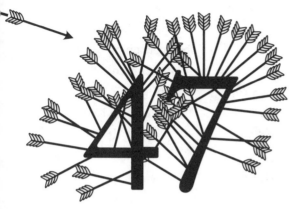

Obsessing over Them

Love is such a powerful force it shouldn't be a surprise when it becomes an obsession. But it's what we do with that obsession that can make our love Cupidity. Not being able to stop thinking about someone is one thing, but a true obsession, according to Merriam-Webster's dictionary, is "a persistent disturbing preoccupation with an often unreasonable idea or feeling." Relational obsessions can come in the form of jealousy, anger, envy, bitterness, or revenge. It might come as a surprise, but letting any of these emotions control you is actually sinful (Romans 8:6-8). Not only are these obsessive tendencies a rejection of God and his Word, but they actually give you the opposite of what they promise. People who act on these emotions have the twisted belief that these actions will return their love and happiness to them. But the truth is that these emotions lead only to destruction and isolation. *Love, by definition, isn't jealous or angry.* It isn't bitter or vengeful (1 Corinthians 13:4-7). So when you start to be fed by those obsessive emotions, love leaves the room. And it's nobody's fault but your own.

Beyond these emotional implications, **obsessing can**

also do spiritual damage. For a time, it can feel like heaven on earth. When the person you love occupies all your thoughts and every spot on your walls, it's a rush. It's like food to the soul, but it's like surviving on a diet comprised solely of Cheetos. Something spiritual is at work, and it ain't good. It's called idolatry. Sure, you might not have a carving of stone made in their likeness tied around your neck, or hey, you might, but that isn't all idolatry is.

> *Letting your sinful nature control your mind leads to death. But letting the Spirit control your mind leads to life and peace. For the sinful nature is always hostile to God. It never did obey God's laws, and it never will. That's why those who are still under the control of their sinful nature can never please God.*
>
> ROMANS 8:6-8

Idolatry is obsessing about anything or anyone other than God himself. Do you have an "immoderate attachment or devotion" to something or someone? Then idol is its name, because that's Merriam-Webster's definition of *idolatry*. Sounds a lot like obsession, doesn't it? Ouch. Hey, we aren't saying it's out of the ordinary to be obsessed when you first fall in love, but we are saying, "Look out." You can't let your obsession last. You've got to get moving and get your mind onto something else (preferably a more worthy object of devotion, if you know what we mean) to ensure that you don't make the pursuit of love your idol. Idolatry is nothing to mess with (Exodus 20:3).

Obsession only serves the obsessor. Because **when you obsess over someone, you smother them**. It's like a puppy on your lap that is licking you incessantly—it might be cute at first, but you can only take so much of it before you need to wipe yourself off and get some space. When you obsess, you often hurt the very object of your obsession, because obsession makes a person crazy. Reactions like jealousy, bitterness, distrust, and a long line of other disgusting emotions can easily follow obsession. Obsession can also cloud your ability to objectively understand social situations. What is really just a simple smile from your love to another person suddenly becomes a sign that they are going to leave you. Or their failure to call you means they are out with someone else. Irrational thoughts lead to irrational relationships. And what happens in most cases is that those compulsive thoughts become self-fulfilling prophecies. In other words, you get what you most fear. Since obsession is a sign that love has gotten off track, it generally leads the one you love to feelings of discomfort and regret. The person they fell in love with was not so focused on their own feelings and fears. But obsession has turned you into a selfish, fearful creature, willing to do whatever it takes to stop what you fear most: losing love.

It's an ironic situation, but obsession serves to run off the very object it's trying to keep hold of. Even if you aren't in a relationship with someone yet but you have found yourself obsessing over them, you are systematically destroying the potential relationship. Instinctually we know that **we are not meant to be worshiped**. It's uncomfortable and unbiblical. So when we run into someone who seems to know everything about us, who says, "God told me to marry you," or who demonstrates any other form of obsession, we want to run away as fast as we can.

If you live with the emotions of jealousy, anger, envy, bitterness, or revenge, you've crossed over into obsession. If you can't stop thinking about someone you aren't dating or someone who has rejected you, you are obsessing. The first thing to do is face the fact that these tendencies are not healthy or God honoring. You can't overlook their negative effects on your life and the life of the other person. The only way out is to switch your obsession from man to God. You've got to get back to the one and only God before your relationships (and your spiritual life) self-destruct.

Five Signs You Might Be Obsessing

+ You are sure God told you to marry them, and you aren't even dating.
+ They said they would call at 9:00; it's 9:10, and you are steaming.
+ You e-mail someone on match.com and tell them that just by reading their profile, you know you're perfect for each other.
+ You're contemplating a tattoo with their name on it to "surprise" them.
+ Your friends haven't heard from you in weeks since you started dating.

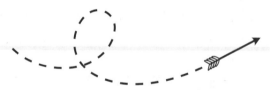

Rehearsing the Other Person's Faults in Your Mind

Whether it's from having unrealistic expectations or from the incompetence of others, it's easy to take what people do wrong (or what you think they're doing wrong) and rehearse it over and over in your mind. Maybe you feel like you've got to complain to somebody but you don't want to be a whiner, so you just shake your head and keep going over the big mess in your mind. The trouble with this kind of thinking is that **God holds us accountable not just for what we do but also for what we think**. He hears your every thought, and each silent, exasperated complaint is like a hotline connected to his ear. None of your thoughts go unnoticed, and no sinful thought goes unpunished—it is virtually the same thing to think something as it is to actually do it (Matthew 5:28). We aren't talking about just the *temptation* to think something here—those thoughts that pop into your mind but you immediately refuse to participate in. Those aren't what pollute the spiritual environment; those are victories. But when you rehearse someone else's sins, or even just their mistakes, over and over in your mind, you commit spiritual Cupidity.

While you might not be able to fully understand the spiritual ramifications of your internal broken record of complaints, you should be able to see the results of this kind of rehearsal on your emotions and attitudes. A woman we know has a problem with anger and shouting at her husband and family. When they don't do what they are supposed to do or when they make a stupid mistake, she pinches her lips together, shakes her head, and thinks things like, *How many times have I told them about this? What were they thinking?!* And then she walks around the house, angrily cleaning up a lost sock here, a dirty lunch plate there, and all the while she is steaming. But one day she got the idea to stop those thoughts as soon as they popped into her head and instead decided to give people the benefit of the doubt. When she did, something changed. Her willingness to make life more about God's law than her own made-up rules brought her freedom. When she majored on empathy and neglected judgment, her tasks of cleaning up after everyone became less burdensome, and her angry outbursts ceased.

Most often, rehearsing other people's faults is a way of expressing judgment. It's the opposite of grace and compassion, and instead it majors on condemnation. It's pointing out the speck in the other person's eye while walking around with a big log in your own (Luke 6:41). So if you've been playing ***the role of the critic***, maybe it's time to just sit back and enjoy the movie without complaining about the acting or the directing.

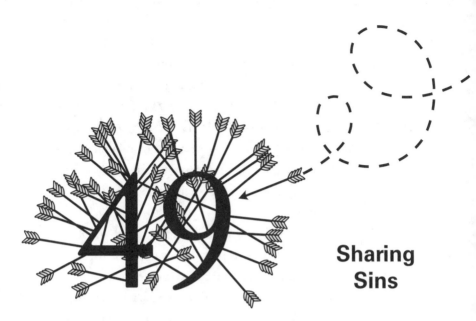

Sharing Sins

True or false: Love means accepting everything, the good and the bad. When someone loves you, you want them to look lovingly on your good parts and look away in ignorant bliss of your blemishes and sinfulness. Ah, twoo wuv! The prevailing mind-set today is, "I want my loved one to take me as I am. I know I've got some dark parts, but I don't want them to remind me. I've got enough problems of my own." That notion is spiritual Cupidity because it assumes our sins are just an inherent part of who we are, like our shoe size, and if they were to be pointed out, that would destroy the love. But if you are letting someone you're in a relationship with encourage your sin, you are living in a spiritual fog. **Love is not complete acceptance of the good and the bad in another person** but a recognition of God's infallibility and your willingness to jump into the fire so the dross will be burned off and you'll be proved good and pure.

The truth is, if anyone is going to notice your sins, both big and small, it ought to be whoever you're in closest relationship with. And if they are privy to all your depravity but aren't saying anything about it, they aren't loving you the way God does. Goodness knows God isn't afraid to call you on your stuff. And he isn't afraid of your wrath. ***In many relationships there is a large rug in the middle of the room with a lot of junk swept under it.*** Sure, the small things—the non-sin and nonessential stuff—should be swept aside and put into the trash. But the sinful stuff that won't fit into the trash bin shouldn't be ignored by you or the one who loves you.

It is an act of spiritual Cupidity to expect someone you love to either share your sinful habits or make allowances for them. Not that it's their job to correct every mistake you ever make, but if you are living in some kind of spiritual darkroom, refusing to shine the light on your favorite sin for fear you'll have to make some changes in your life, then you're blind to truth. And love doesn't encourage darkness but light (1 John 2:9-11).

If you are dating someone right now who encourages your sin or participates in it with you, they aren't truly loving you—at least not as God would have them love you. And if you are married to someone who does the same, it's time for some sober discussion about your unspoken agreement to turn your backs on God.

In the case of a man who makes this realization before his wife, he must quickly act on it and bring restoration to his home. Paul makes this mandatory for Christian leaders as well (1 Timothy 3:4-5). If you are a wife, your job is slightly different, because to attempt to direct your husband out of the darkness is to take the lead. It is up to a woman to take responsibility for her own role in shared sin, regardless of how her husband responds. ***She may not be able to change his behavior, but she can change her own.*** He might notice the transformation in her and become convicted himself, but if it doesn't happen that way, she must not become angry or take matters into her own hands. She needs to pray for her husband and trust that the God who restores has the ability to speak to him as well as to her.

When you realize there is sin in your life, it is never okay to commit another sin in an attempt to fix things. Sin—of any kind—always makes things worse. And although we all learned good lessons about sharing in kindergarten, sin is sort of like a used Kleenex—it's just one of those things you don't want to pass around.

Not Knowing What True Love Is

The woman had an inferiority complex. She hated herself, some might say. And so it seemed that all her relationships were disastrous, leaving nothing but the backsides of fearful men running from her. *She might as well have been Godzilla tiptoeing through the china shop of love.* "You need to love yourself before you can love a man," her best friend said.

Like this friend, many a well-meaning person has told a confused soul that they couldn't love anyone because they didn't love themselves. And while that sounds really good, it is actually spiritual Cupidity. "What?" you say. "I've heard that many times, and it totally makes sense. After all, if you hate yourself, where will you find the strength to love?" You can make all kinds of arguments that sound very wise and even quasi-biblical to support this idea, but we have to be careful that our standard of truth is God's Word, not popular culture. When you are born and raised in a certain culture, it becomes easy to adopt that culture, even when you don't want to—or you don't even realize it. Whenever you hear something or believe something, test it against God's Word. In this case, the concept is love. So let's take a look at biblical love and see if we can find out what true love is.

The two greatest commandments both involve love. So if any conditions would apply to your ability to love, it would make sense that they would show up there. Let's have a look: "The most important commandment is this: 'Listen, O Israel! The LORD our God is the one and only LORD. And you must love the LORD your God with all your heart, all your soul, all your mind, and all your strength.' The second is equally important: 'Love your neighbor as yourself.' No other commandment is greater than these" (Mark 12:29-31). Notice the order of these two commandments. First, love God with everything that is in you, and then love others as you love yourself.

Now some of you might be saying, "See! Love others as you love *yourself.*" But don't miss what Jesus says about how we must love God. With *all* your heart, with *all* your soul, with *all* your mind, and with *all* your strength. So no less than 100 percent! And how are we to love others? Scripture doesn't say with 100 percent of our being, does it? It simply says to love others *as you love yourself*—not less than you love yourself. The thing to note is that these commandments are not commands to love yourself but to love God with everything you have and love others no less than you love yourself. God doesn't have to command us to love ourselves, because that part comes naturally to humans (Ephesians 5:29). He reveals to us that the way to show love to ourselves is by loving others (Ephesians 5:28).

So if Jesus doesn't talk about loving yourself, other than not to love others less than yourself, where do we get the whole "you have to love yourself" mantra? Secular psychology, of course. The discipline of psychology focuses solely on studying and improving *self* and was developed by nonbelievers. Taking the liberty of putting words in the mouths of the founding fathers of psychology like Freud, Skinner, Jung, and their ilk, here is psychology's version of the two greatest commandments: "The most important commandment is this: 'Listen, O modern nations! You are the one and only lord. And you must love yourself with all your heart, all your soul, all your mind, and all your strength.' The second is only important after following the first: 'Love your neighbor almost as much as yourself but never more than yourself.'" You see, in psychology, self is god. But that's a far cry from Jesus' description of love. In John 15:12 Jesus says, "This is my commandment: Love each other in the same way I have loved you." Notice that this love is based not on how you feel about yourself but on how Jesus loves you. We can never love anyone better than that. Biblically mandated love is never based on conditions, as in "Love others once _____ happens." Real love is never that fickle or shallow. It is a command, and as no one can command a feeling, you can be sure the love God calls us to isn't a mushy, I-adore-you-because-of-the-way-I-feel kind of love; it's a conscious act of your will to treat others in love.

When we start putting conditions on love, we know the world has crept into our theology. If we believe we can't love others until we love ourselves, God's command is useless—how can he command you to do something today that isn't possible until you get another condition settled? In 1 John, love is explained like this: "We should love one another.... If we love our Christian brothers and sisters, it proves that we have passed from death to life. But a person who has no love is still dead" (1 John 3:11, 14). ***Waiting to love others for any reason is a dangerous choice.*** In 1 John 4:7-8 we are hit with another command to love: "Let us continue to love one another, for love comes from God. Anyone who loves is a child of God and knows God. But anyone who does not love does not know God, for God is love." That should clear things up—sounds like our ability to love comes from God. When we accept the Spirit of God into our lives, we gain the ability to love, for God is love. Again, it has nothing to do with how much we love ourselves but how much he loves us. "This is real love—not that we loved God, but that he loved us and sent his Son as a sacrifice to take away our sins. Dear friends, since God loved us that much, we surely ought to love each other. No one has ever seen God. But if we love each other, God lives in us, and his love is brought to full expression in us" (1 John 4:10-12). Why do we love? Because God loved us. How do we love? God's way. When do we love? Always.

> *This is real love—not that we loved God, but that he loved us and sent his Son as a sacrifice to take away our sins. Dear friends, since God loved us that much, we surely ought to love each other. No one has ever seen God. But if we love each other, God lives in us, and his love is brought to full expression in us.*
>
> 1 JOHN 4:10-12

This is the kind of work we should do whenever we find that we are accepting a certain way of living—take what we believe and test it against God's Word. The role of self in the way we love might seem like a subtle nuance, but each nuance that sets itself up in opposition to God's Word allows the culture to integrate itself more and more into our lives. It desensitizes us to lies and keeps Scripture at arm's length. As followers of Christ, we cannot allow the world to lie to us. We cannot take those lies and call them truth, not even for a moment. We need to refuse what sounds good to our flesh but can't be supported by Scripture, especially when it keeps us from acting on God's Word. If you believed you had to love yourself before you could love others, then you might put off God's command to love others until you felt like you loved yourself. How long is it okay to put off God's commands? A day? A week? God indicates that no delay is acceptable: "If you listen to the word and don't obey, it is like glancing at your face in a mirror. You see yourself, walk away, and forget what you look like. But if you look carefully into the perfect law that sets you free, and if you do what it says and don't forget what you heard, then God will bless you for doing it" (James 1:23-25).

As we talked about at the beginning of this book, true love isn't a feeling but a chance to share the love God has given you with others. ***True love isn't about getting but giving.*** It isn't about keeping track of wrongs but mending rights. True love doesn't always feel good and mushy; sometimes it confronts and challenges our sin nature. But it's always the best choice. And that's the point: love is a choice, not an emotion. Understand that, and you will understand true love.

If you are in a relationship that isn't working, if the self-loathing you feel or your partner feels is the source of discord and trauma, then the answer isn't to start some self-esteem or self-love therapy. It's time to get into God's Word and find out who God is and who you are in relation to him. Waiting until you overcome your demons or heal your old wounds before stopping your cycle of sin is just an excuse to avoid the hard work of sanctification. There are always obstacles to cutting out sin, but those obstacles should never be used as rationalizations or things to hide behind. You've heard the truth, and now there are no excuses.

Simply put, love comes from above, not from inside. With God's help, you can do this. Let's not allow the world to dilute our faith. Refuse to integrate concepts of yourself as god, as the most important being, into your way of living. Test everything against God's Word. Refuse to passively accept cultural norms, even cultural norms that are passed off as "Christian." Let it be your goal to obey God's Word instantly and always. When you do, you will have **more love than you know what to do with**.

$$\ggg\!\!\longrightarrow$$

At the risk of pointing out the obvious, spiritual acts of Cupidity are the dullest, slowest, and dumbest of all the types. They result from knowing what God's Word says and deciding to go against it anyway in an attempt to get love. Huh? Knock, knock, is anyone home? Fear, worry, loneliness, anger, and any number of other powerful emotions can scream louder than truth and get you thinking all kinds of insanity, but don't strap on the straitjacket just yet. You aren't alone in your inability to do what you know is right. "I don't really understand myself, for I want to do what is right, but I don't do it. Instead, I do what I hate" (Romans 7:15). Sound familiar? It's an age-old problem, one not even the greatest spiritual leaders in the world have conquered. But that doesn't mean they stop trying; it just means they don't beat themselves up over it. Thank God there is no condemnation for those who are in Christ Jesus (Romans 8:1).

It's easy to say that because we've messed up so much, because we are so bad at love, we ought to just give up trying. But that would be the greatest act of spiritual Cupidity around, because the entire law and the demands of all the prophets are based on the choice to love God and those *crazy yet lovable human beings* of his. Saying love is just too hard and that you're taking a pass is to take a pass on faith, on God, and on truth. You just can't do it. So what's left but an uncomfortable resolution to keep asking yourself, *Why? Why am I acting like this? Why do I think they ought to do this or that? Why am I afraid? Why can't I obey?* The questions that get you to look at the sin in your life are the questions that are going to knock the Cupidity right out of you. It's the lazy acceptance of the status quo that makes love suffer.

There is no one righteous, not even one (Romans 3:10). So why pretend everything is perfect when it isn't? "If we claim we have no sin, we are only fooling ourselves and not living in the truth. But if we confess our sins to him, he is faithful and just to forgive us our sins and to cleanse us from all wickedness. If we claim we have not sinned, we are calling God a liar and showing that his word has no place in our hearts" (1 John 1:8-10). That's not to say you have to find a ghost behind every door or a skeleton in every closet—where do you live, a haunted house? But you do have to continually reflect on how comfortable you've gotten with sin and how much you've let the ideas of the world become a part of your way of thinking. Just because Oprah said it, that doesn't make it true. (Unless she said, "Buy *Cupidity*—it's a great book!") And just because it can feel like a psychologically dangerous procedure to give up looking out for number one and deciding instead to look out for others, that doesn't make it any less biblical.

The End

The End of Cupidity

The end of Cupidity comes when love is defined not only as godly but as God himself (1 John 4:16). You would never reject God, so why would you reject the very thing that defines him as well as your own faith? To know the truth and not to live by it—in other words, to not believe it—is to be an unbeliever. "Don't just listen to God's word. You must do what it says. Otherwise, you are only fooling yourselves" (James 1:22). Confidence, not doubt, is your weapon against Cupidity—confidence that God and his commands are all you need not only to love but to live (John 6:35).

Cupidity is believing what the world says about love even though it completely contradicts God's Word. We hope that this book has shed some light on some of the utter Cupidity in your past and that as a result you are making changes to retrain your mind, heart, and body in the way of truth. **Cupidity doesn't have to be a way of life for you any longer.** Starting today, you can make changes that will rescue you from future blunders of faith and love.

Beyond that, it is also important to accept the fact that you might have messed up in the past and not loved the way God calls you to. When you can spot your mistakes and confess them, you can start to get free from them. "Finally, I confessed all my sins to you and stopped trying to hide my guilt. I said to myself, 'I will confess my rebellion to the Lord.' And you forgave me! All my guilt is gone" (Psalm 32:5). The beginning of confession is the end of Cupidity.

We hope this book has given you enough to think about in relation to your relationship. And we hope it is leading you to excitement at the prospect of cleaning up the Cupidity in your life. No one lives in a world fully free of self-induced Cupidity, not even us. But don't let that stop you from purging as much of it as you can. Like we tell our daughter, "How do you eat an elephant? One bite at a time." Get to work making Cupidity an occasional footnote in your relationship instead of the recurring theme of your autobiography!

About the Authors

Hayley DiMarco is the best-selling author of more than thirty books, including *Dateable, Marriable, Mean Girls,* and *The Woman of Mystery.* She spent the early part of her career working for a little shoe company called Nike in Portland, Oregon, and Thomas Nelson publishing in Nashville, Tennessee.

In 2002 Hayley left Nelson and founded Hungry Planet, a company intensely focused on feeding the world's appetite for truth by producing books and new media, taking on issues of faith and life with a distinctly modern voice.

Shortly after founding Hungry Planet, Hayley successfully completed a nationwide executive search for someone to run the company so she could focus on writing. She describes her husband, Michael, as her most successful business acquisition! In addition to the nine books he has authored or coauthored, Michael also created The Hungry Planet Bible Project, a ten thousand–mile road trip designed to give a voice to the hungry and homeless.

Hayley and Michael are the proud parents of dozens of Hungry Planet books—including eleven best sellers, four ECPA Christian Book Award finalists, and one ECPA winner—and one amazing human, their daughter, Addison.

Find out more about Hungry Planet at www.hungryplanet-books.com and The Hungry Planet Bible Project at www.hpbp .org. And join in the Cupidity conversation at www.babbleofthe sexes.com!

Hungry Planet

Feeding the world's appetite for truth.

- Nine straight titles on the CBA young adult bestseller list
- More than 800,000 books in print
- Three finalists and one winner of the ECPA Christian Book Awards

After all this and more, Hungry Planet has established itself as the leading provider of books for teens and not-yet-old adults. Dedicated to creating relevant, spiritually based books, Hungry Planet delivers honest, in-your-face truth and twenty-first-century application within a visually engaging package no reader can forget.

www.hungryplanetbooks.com

CP0377